LAYERS OF LEARNING
YEAR FOUR • UNIT FOURTEEN

ISRAEL
APPALACHIAN STATES
CHEMISTRY OF FARMING
MODERN MUSIC

Published by HooDoo Publishing
United States of America
© 2017 Layers of Learning
(Grilled Cheese BTN Font) © Fontdiner - www.fontdiner.com
ISBN #978-1548532246

Units at a Glance: Topics For All Four Years of the Layers of Learning Program

1	History	Geography	Science	The Arts
1	Mesopotamia	Maps & Globes	Planets	Cave Paintings
2	Egypt	Map Keys	Stars	Egyptian Art
3	Europe	Global Grids	Earth & Moon	Crafts
4	Ancient Greece	Wonders	Satellites	Greek Art
5	Babylon	Mapping People	Humans in Space	Poetry
6	The Levant	Physical Earth	Laws of Motion	List Poems
7	Phoenicians	Oceans	Motion	Moral Stories
8	Assyrians	Deserts	Fluids	Rhythm
9	Persians	Arctic	Waves	Melody
10	Ancient China	Forests	Machines	Chinese Art
11	Early Japan	Mountains	States of Matter	Line & Shape
12	Arabia	Rivers & Lakes	Atoms	Color & Value
13	Ancient India	Grasslands	Elements	Texture & Form
14	Ancient Africa	Africa	Bonding	African Tales
15	First North Americans	North America	Salts	Creative Kids
16	Ancient South America	South America	Plants	South American Art
17	Celts	Europe	Flowering Plants	Jewelry
18	Roman Republic	Asia	Trees	Roman Art
19	Christianity	Australia & Oceania	Simple Plants	Instruments
20	Roman Empire	You Explore	Fungi	Composing Music

2	History	Geography	Science	The Arts
1	Byzantines	Turkey	Climate & Seasons	Byzantine Art
2	Barbarians	Ireland	Forecasting	Illumination
3	Islam	Arabian Peninsula	Clouds & Precipitation	Creative Kids
4	Vikings	Norway	Special Effects	Viking Art
5	Anglo Saxons	Britain	Wild Weather	King Arthur Tales
6	Charlemagne	France	Cells & DNA	Carolingian Art
7	Normans	Nigeria	Skeletons	Canterbury Tales
8	Feudal System	Germany	Muscles, Skin, Cardio	Gothic Art
9	Crusades	Balkans	Digestive & Senses	Religious Art
10	Burgundy, Venice, Spain	Switzerland	Nerves	Oil Paints
11	Wars of the Roses	Russia	Health	Minstrels & Plays
12	Eastern Europe	Hungary	Metals	Printmaking
13	African Kingdoms	Mali	Carbon Chemistry	Textiles
14	Asian Kingdoms	Southeast Asia	Non-metals	Vivid Language
15	Mongols	Caucasus	Gases	Fun With Poetry
16	Medieval China & Japan	China	Electricity	Asian Arts
17	Pacific Peoples	Micronesia	Circuits	Arts of the Islands
18	American Peoples	Canada	Technology	Indian Legends
19	The Renaissance	Italy	Magnetism	Renaissance Art I
20	Explorers	Caribbean Sea	Motors	Renaissance Art II

3	History	Geography	Science	The Arts
1	Age of Exploration	Argentina & Chile	Classification & Insects	Fairy Tales
2	The Ottoman Empire	Egypt & Libya	Reptiles & Amphibians	Poetry
3	Mogul Empire	Pakistan & Afghanistan	Fish	Mogul Arts
4	Reformation	Angola & Zambia	Birds	Reformation Art
5	Renaissance England	Tanzania & Kenya	Mammals & Primates	Shakespeare
6	Thirty Years' War	Spain	Sound	Baroque Music
7	The Dutch	Netherlands	Light & Optics	Baroque Art I
8	France	Indonesia	Bending Light	Baroque Art II
9	The Enlightenment	Korean Peninsula	Color	Art Journaling
10	Russia & Prussia	Central Asia	History of Science	Watercolors
11	Conquistadors	Baltic States	Igneous Rocks	Creative Kids
12	Settlers	Peru & Bolivia	Sedimentary Rocks	Native American Art
13	13 Colonies	Central America	Metamorphic Rocks	Settler Sayings
14	Slave Trade	Brazil	Gems & Minerals	Colonial Art
15	The South Pacific	Australasia	Fossils	Principles of Art
16	The British in India	India	Chemical Reactions	Classical Music
17	The Boston Tea Party	Japan	Reversible Reactions	Folk Music
18	Founding Fathers	Iran	Compounds & Solutions	Rococo
19	Declaring Independence	Samoa & Tonga	Oxidation & Reduction	Creative Crafts I
20	The American Revolution	South Africa	Acids & Bases	Creative Crafts II

4	History	Geography	Science	The Arts
1	American Government	USA	Heat & Temperature	Patriotic Music
2	Expanding Nation	Pacific States	Motors & Engines	Tall Tales
3	Industrial Revolution	U.S. Landscapes	Energy	Romantic Art I
4	Revolutions	Mountain West States	Energy Sources	Romantic Art II
5	Africa	U.S. Political Maps	Energy Conversion	Impressionism I
6	The West	Southwest States	Earth Structure	Impressionism II
7	Civil War	National Parks	Plate Tectonics	Post Impressionism
8	World War I	Plains States	Earthquakes	Expressionism
9	Totalitarianism	U.S. Economics	Volcanoes	Abstract Art
10	Great Depression	Heartland States	Mountain Building	Kinds of Art
11	World War II	Symbols & Landmarks	Chemistry of Air & Water	War Art
12	Modern East Asia	The South	Food Chemistry	Modern Art
13	India's Independence	People of America	Industry	Pop Art
14	Israel	Appalachian States	Chemistry of Farming	Modern Music
15	Cold War	U.S. Territories	Chemistry of Medicine	Free Verse
16	Vietnam War	Atlantic States	Food Chains	Photography
17	Latin America	New England States	Animal Groups	Latin American Art
18	Civil Rights	Home State Study I	Instincts	Theater & Film
19	Technology	Home State Study II	Habitats	Architecture
20	Terrorism	America in Review	Conservation	Creative Kids

Unit 4-14

Printable Pack

This unit includes printables at the end. To make life easier for you we also created digital printable packs for each unit. To retrieve your printable pack for Unit 4-14, please visit

www.layers-of-learning.com/digital-printable-packs/

Put the printable pack in your shopping cart and use this coupon code:

621UNIT4-14

Your printable pack will be free.

Layers of Learning Introduction

This is part of a series of units in the Layers of Learning homeschool curriculum, including the subjects of history, geography, science, and the arts. Children from 1st through 12th can participate in the same curriculum at the same time - family school style.

The units are intended to be used in order as the basis of a complete curriculum (once you add in a systematic math, reading, and writing program). You begin with Year 1 Unit 1 no matter what ages your children are. Spend about 2 weeks on each unit. You pick and choose the activities within the unit that appeal to you and read the books from the book list that are available to you or find others on the same topic from your library. We highly recommend that you use the timeline in every history section as the backbone. Then flesh out your learning with reading and activities that highlight the topics you think are the most important.

Alternatively, you can use the units as activity ideas to supplement another curriculum in any order you wish. You can still use them with all ages of children at the same time.

When you've finished with Year One, move on to Year Two, Year Three, and Year Four. Then begin again with Year One and work your way through the years again. Now your children will be older, reading more involved books, and writing more in depth. When you have completed the sequence for the second time, you start again on it for the third and final time. If your student began with Layers of Learning in 1st grade and stayed with it all the way through she would go through the four year rotation three times, firmly cementing the information in her mind in ever increasing depth. At each level you should expect increasing amounts of outside reading and writing. High schoolers in particular should be reading extensively, and if possible, participating in discussion groups.

These icons will guide you in spotting activities and books that are appropriate for the age of child you are working with. But if you think an activity is too juvenile or too difficult for your kids, adjust accordingly. The icons are not there as rules, just guides.

☺ 1st-4th
☻ 5th-8th
☻ 9th-12th

Within each unit we share:

EXPLORATIONS, activities relating to the topic;
EXPERIMENTS, usually associated with science topics;
EXPEDITIONS, field trips;
EXPLANATIONS, teacher helps or educational philosophies.

In the sidebars we also include Additional Layers, Famous Folks, Fabulous Facts, On the Web, and other extra related topics that can take you off on tangents, exploring the world and your interests with a bit more freedom. The curriculum will always be there to pull you back on track when you're ready.

www.layers-of-learning.com

UNIT FOURTEEN

ISRAEL - APPALACHIAN STATES - CHEMISTRY OF FARMING - MODERN MUSIC

Writing is perhaps the greatest of human inventions, binding together people who never knew each other, citizens of distant epochs. Books break the shackles of time. A book is proof that humans are capable of working magic.

-Carl Sagan, American astrophysicist

LIBRARY LIST

HISTORY	Search for: Israel, Zionism, David Ben-Gurion, Six Day War, Yom Kippur War

Search for: Israel, Zionism, David Ben-Gurion, Six Day War, Yom Kippur War

☺ This is Israel by Miroslav Sasek.

☺ Let's Visit Jerusalem! by Lisa Manzione.

☺ Children of Israel by Lauri M. Grossman.

☺ ☻ Welcome to Israel by Lilly Rivlin and Gila Gevirtz. History, politics, culture, and geography all in one.

☺ ☻ Israel: Repairing the World by Rabbi Stephen Wise. The accomplishments of Jews and the nation of Israel.

☺ ☻ Israel by Elaine Landau.

☻ Understanding Israel by Sol Scharfstein. History of the modern state.

☻ Ben Gurion: Builder of Israel by Robert St. John.

☺ ☻ Displaced Persons: The Liberation and Abuse of Holocaust Survivors by Ted Gottfried. Discusses the antisemitism that led up to the Holocaust and the continuance of this dangerous racism today.

☺ ☻ The Creation of Israel by Jim Whiting. Perfect digest of the highlights.

☺ ☻ Homeland by Marv Wolfman, Mario Ruiz, William J. Rubin. Graphic history of Israel from ancient times to the present. The whole scope is important.

☺ ☻ A Promise Fulfilled by Howard Greenfield.

☺ ☻ Theodor Herzl by Norman G. Finkelstein. Biography of one of the founders of Israel.

☻ Israel: A History by Martin Gilbert. Long; read at least up to the formation of Israel.

☻ The Case For Israel by Allan Dershowitz. Makes the case for why we should be pro-Israel.

☻ A History of the Jews by Paul Johnson. Covers 4,000 years of Jewish history from the perspective of a Christian. Perfect for seeing the whole scope of Israel's importance.

☻ Start-up Nation: The Story of Israel's Economic Miracle by Dan Senor & Saul Singer.

GEOGRAPHY	Search for: Tennessee, Kentucky, West Virginia, Virginia, North Carolina ☺ <u>V is for Volunteer: A Tennessee Alphabet</u> by Michael Shoulders. ☺ <u>B is for Bluegrass: A Kentucky Alphabet</u> by Mary Ann McCabe Riehle. ☺ <u>M is for Mountain State: A West Virginia Alphabet</u> by Mary Ann McCabe Rielhe. ☺ <u>When I Was Young in the Mountains</u> by Cynthia Rylant. About West Virginia. ☺ <u>O is For Old Dominion: A Virginia Alphabet</u> by Pamela Duncan Edwards. ☺ <u>T is for Tar Heel: A North Carolina Alphabet</u> by Carol Crane. ☺ ☻ <u>Tennessee</u> by Myra S. Weatherly. ☺ ☻ <u>West Virginia</u> by Barbara A. Somervill. ☻ <u>Kentucky</u> by Andrew Santella. ☺ ☻ <u>Tennessee</u> by Deborah Kent. ☻ <u>North Carolina</u> by Tanya Lloyd Kyi. Look for other titles in this "America" series. ☻ <u>The Story of Kentucky</u> by Rice S. Eubank. Written in 1913. Free Kindle version.
SCIENCE	Search for: farming, fertilizers, pesticides, chemistry of farming ☺ <u>Plants on a Farm</u> by Nancy Dickmann. ☺ <u>Milk: From Cow to Carton</u> by Aliki. ☺ <u>Garbage Helps Our Garden Grow</u> by Linda Glaser. About composting. ☺ ☻ <u>Nitrogen</u> by Salvatore Tocci. Nitrogen is an important element in soil for plants. ☺ ☻ <u>Critical Thinking About Pesticides</u> by Samantha Beres. Gives different points of view and the facts behind the controversy. ☻ <u>Know Soil, Know Life</u> by David L. Lindbow. Especially relevant is Chapter 4. ☻ <u>Gardening For Geeks</u> by Christy Wilhelmi. Focus on the science sections.
THE ARTS	Search for: modern music, jazz, musicals, rock and roll, other specific genres or musicians you are interested in. Check the biography shelf in the children's section of your library and find a recent musician's story to read. ☺ <u>The Music in George's Head: George Gershwin Creates Rhapsody in Blue</u> by Suzanne Slade. This is a picture book that shows how Gershwin combined styles to make new kinds of music. ☺ <u>The Jazz Fly</u> by Matthew Gollub. A fly demonstrates improvisation and jazz scat by using the sounds of other animals he hears. Comes with a CD. ☺ ☻ <u>Jazz on a Saturday Night</u> by Leo & Diane Dillon. Picture book also comes with a CD of jazz music and a demonstration of what each jazz instrument sounds like. ☺ ☻ <u>Elvis: The Story of the Rock and Roll King</u> by Bonnie Christensen. ☺ ☻ <u>What is Rock and Roll?</u> by Jim O'Connor and Gregory Copeland. ☺ ☻ <u>The Beatles</u> by Mike Venezia. This is part of the Getting to Know The World's Greatest Composers Series. Look for more. Gershwin, Duke Ellington, and other modern musicians all have books in this series. ☺ ☻ <u>Say It With Music: The Story of Irving Berlin</u> by Nancy Furstinger. Look for others in the Modern Music Masters series as well. Michael Jackson, Leonard Bernstein, Bob Marley, James Brown, and more all have books within the series.

HISTORY: ISRAEL

Additional Layer

Israel has no oil and no precious metals or gems. It is a tiny strip of land along the eastern coast of the Mediterranean. It is dry and hot and not particularly pretty. But everybody seems to want it. In fact, many people are perfectly willing to kill and exterminate entire populations in order to get it. As you study this unit see if you can find out why.

Fabulous Fact

Palestine was the name the Romans gave the province that included Israel and the rest of the eastern shore of the Mediterranean. Arab and Turkish Muslims, Christians, and Jews have all lived there since ancient times.

Palestine has never been a nation and it is not a race. It is the name that modern Arabs who live in Israel and the bordering regions call themselves, since they do not feel they have a nation of their own.

Israel began its modern life in the late 1800s. Jews had been persecuted and driven from every nation in Europe, most of Asia, and northern Africa at some point over the last two millennia, sometimes repeatedly. Jews were barred entry from most South American nations. Their immigration, even to the United States, was sharply controlled since the earliest days of the colonies. A few well-educated Jews in leadership realized that the only way their people could have peace would be if they could have a nation of their own and become strong enough to defend their borders, which they had no doubt would be eternally necessary.

This is the famed Western Wall in Jerusalem. It is the only part of the ancient temple of Solomon still standing. Jews go there to pray. Before 1965 the wall was in Palestinian-held territory, and Jews were barred from visiting. Photo by Wayne McLean and shared under CC license.

Zionism means a reestablishment of the Jewish people to their ancient homeland of Jerusalem. The new movement of Zionism began to gain some traction and a following among Jews, but no interest whatsoever from the international community.

During World War I the Ottoman Empire, which controlled the Levant at the time, sided with Germany against Russia, England, and France. When the Ottomans lost the war they also lost their empire, and the Holy Land came to be controlled by the British and the French. Jews and Christians had been living in the region since ancient times, but were always treated badly by their Muslim masters. Now they saw new hope with Western European nations at the helm. But the British were extremely anxious to appease and please their new subjects to avoid uprisings in a land where they could spare few troops. As part of that appeasement, the British denied the entry of Jews who wished to immigrate to their ancient homeland.

As the Germans became more and more aggressive and began to discriminate against the Jews and destroy their civil liberties in the 1930s, Jews searched for a place to flee to. All doors were closed. America only allowed a trickle of immigrants. The remaining countries of the West were no better. A few Jews disregarded the laws and immigrated to the Holy Land illegally, but most were trapped with no place to flee to until it was too late. In the aftermath of World War II, as the full extent of the horror of the Holocaust became plain, first the British and then the French and the Americans championed a plan to give the Jews a homeland where they could have the political power and the freedom to defend themselves. It was plain to all that no one else could be depended on to defend the Jews.

During World War II the Arab states had risen up in rebellion and fought on the side of the Nazis. They had forfeited their rights as citizens of the British Empire and were treated as conquered people. In 1948, just after the State of Israel was created, war broke out between the Jews and the Arabs. The Jews won. Around 750,000 Palestinian Arabs were either forced to leave or flee their homes.

The first Jews to pour into Israel were the homeless, the destitute, and the thousands upon thousands of orphan refugees from the horror of post-World War II Europe. Others, more prosperous and whole, came from America, Canada, England, South America, and Russia.

The early leaders of Israel worked tirelessly to build a new nation based on the republican models of England and the United States. They were determined to care for the hundred thousand refugees that overwhelmed their resources and to build a modern infrastructure of roads and power and ports. They were also extremely preoccupied with their military. They were surrounded on every side by hostile people who they knew they had to defend themselves against.

From those early days up until today, Israel has prospered economically. In very few years they have become one of the greatest economic powerhouses in the world. Their people are prosperous and strong. And they continue to this day to fight for their lives against the hatred and discrimination they have endured.

Fabulous Fact

No one really knows the cause of the Palestinian Exodus of 1948. Pro-Arab people believe the Jews forcibly drove the Arabs out. Pro-Israel people say the Arabs either left on their own or were ordered out by their own leaders. Possibly it was a combination of the two.

It matters because people in the Holy Land today are still trying to figure out who should own the land and what should be done about it. If the Arabs left voluntarily, then they forfeited some of their rights, but if they were driven out, then the opposite is true.

Additional Layer

Israel could not have fed her refugee population in those early years without private charity donations reaching the millions, mostly from America.

Fabulous Fact

The British and the UN partitioned the Holy Land into Arab held Palestine and Jewish held Israel in 1948, giving the Arabs their own legal nation. But they were immediately annexed by Egypt and Jordan.

Famous Folks

Yitzhak Rabin, the commander of the Israeli military during the Six-Day War gave the war the name, invoking the six days of creation.

Rabin later became one of Israel's most revered Prime Ministers. He was assassinated in office in 1995 by an Israeli radical who opposed the Oslo Accords of peace between Israel and Arafat, the leader of the Palestinian people.

Fabulous Fact

The Israelis invented the Uzi sub-machine gun for their military in the 1950s. It is the best selling sub-machine gun of all time.

☺ ☺ ☻ EXPLORATION: Timeline

At the end of this unit you will find printable timeline squares. Cut the squares out and place them on a wall timeline or in a notebook timeline. These work best when used with the timeline squares from other units so you can see what is happening at different places of the world at the same time.

☺ ☻ EXPLORATION: Israel's Flag

Israel's flag has two horizontal blue stripes and a blue Star of David on a white background. The design is intended to remind people of the Jewish prayer shawls which are white with blue along the borders. The color blue has been used since ancient times to remind the people of the covenants they made with God.

This is a painting of a rabbi with a prayer shawl by Isidor Kaufmann.

The Star of David has been a Jewish symbol since at least the 1500s (probably much earlier). It has come to be an internationally recognized symbol of the Jews as a race and political group as well as the Jewish religion.

Finger paint a Jewish flag. Start with a sheet of white freezer paper. Paint the blue details with this homemade finger paint:

- 2 Tbsp. sugar
- 1/3 cup cornstarch
- 2 cups cold water
- ¼ cup clear dishwashing liquid
- blue food coloring

Mix sugar and cornstarch in a small saucepan. Add water, and whisk together until smooth. Heat over medium heat until thickened. Remove from heat and stir in the dishwashing liquid. Add blue food coloring until the colors are vibrant.

☻ EXPLORATION: Zionism

Zionism is the movement for a Jewish homeland in the Holy Land. The modern movement began in the late 1800s among Jews in central and eastern Europe. But Jews had been longing for their homeland since they were taken captive by Babylon in 586 BC. Read Psalm 137 from the Old Testament. It is a lament for Israel.

Next, look up "My Heart Is in the East" by Judah HaLevi, a Spanish Jew who lived during the time of the Islamic occupation of Spain. The poem expresses a desire for Israel, a place of home for the Jews.

Finally, read through the Wikipedia article, "Jewish Refugees."
https://en.wikipedia.org/wiki/Jewish_refugees

As you read, use the printable map from the end of this unit and make tally marks in the box for each of the regions, one for each time the Jews were expelled, severely persecuted, or driven from a place in that region. Some of the entries mention more than one region or more than one expulsion, put a tally mark for each region and each occurrence.

After studying the history of expulsions of the Jews you should be able to see the appeal of a Jewish homeland, a political place from which the Jews could defend themselves and never be driven out again.

☻ ☻ ☻ EXPLORATION: David Ben-Gurion

David Ben-Gurion became the foremost leader in the Zionist movement to create an Israeli homeland. He also served as the first Israeli Prime Minister and is considered the founding father of Israel.

Research more about David Ben-Gurion. Write a biography and tell about the events of his life. Younger kids can color and fill out the facts on the printable about David Ben-Gurion from the end of this unit.

Additional Layer

People who support Zionism believe it protects and repatriates a persecuted people. People who are against the movement believe it is racist, colonialist, and persecutes Palestinian Arabs.

Read both sides of the story before you develop an opinion.

Fabulous Fact

The Jewish Agency For Israel was founded in 1929 with the purpose of inspiring Jews to have a desire to reclaim their ancient homeland in Israel. The agency also worked to convince nations that the Jews ought to have a homeland where they could dwell safely from persecution. The agency still exists today and works to inspire a sense of community and pride in Israel among Jews from around the world.

Additional Layer

Israel is believed to have nuclear weapons, but no one knows for sure. Israel isn't telling.

If you were Israel, would you want nuclear weapons in your situation? Would you want to keep them a secret?

Fabulous Fact

Israel is tiny. It is just over 8,000 square miles, a little smaller than the state of New Jersey. At its widest point it is just 71 miles and at its narrowest only 9 miles. It is 263 miles from north to south.

Additional Layer

In the early years of Israel the Kibbutz system was very popular. New settlers would give up all their possessions and social status, and even their families to a certain extent, and live communally in a communist-equality utopia. Kids were raised away from their parents, who spent several hours a day with them, but did not educate, discipline, or protect them; this was done by the community. Women and men were treated the same and given similar jobs and educations. Find out what happened to the Kibbutz system and whether it still exists today.

When and where have other utopian plans been implemented? What were the results of those experiments?

☺ ☺ ☺ EXPLORATION: Six-Day War

In 1967 Egypt was growing increasingly belligerent. They closed down the shipping lanes in the Straits of Tiran. They committed acts of terrorism against Israeli civilians and sabotage against the Israeli military. They amassed troops and planes along the Israeli border in the Sinai and ordered out UN peacekeeping troops. The Syrians and Jordanians joined Egyptian aggression and also amassed troops.

On June 5th Israel launched a surprise attack on Egyptian, Jordanian, and Syrian airfields, completely destroying them. They then attacked by land, pushing back the armies of all three nations. Israel took the entire Sinai Peninsula, the Golan Heights, the West Bank, the city of Jerusalem, and the Gaza Strip. By June 10th the war was over. Egypt, Syria, and Jordan were utterly defeated. Israel's territory had tripled.

The war showed that Israel was not defenseless or weak. The rapid conclusion and decisiveness of the victory has kept the Middle East wary of Israel ever since.

Color the map of the Six-Day War from the end of this unit.

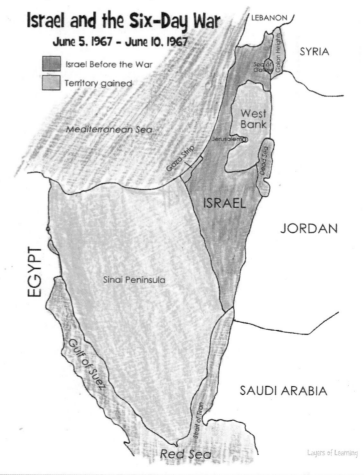

Discuss Israel's use of a preemptive strike. This tactic is widely disputed in the world today. Is it justified to attack an obviously aggressive force, or must you wait for their attack? Would such action be justified in your personal life? For example, would it be okay to take action if a bully were threatening you or your family?

☺ EXPLORATION: Yom Kippur War
Watch "Yom Kippur war - Israel fights for her life and wins" on YouTube: https://www.youtube.com/watch?v=Xrlboylx9Jo

As you watch take notes on a piece of paper, divided vertically into two sides. One side should be for Egypt and Syria and the other for Israel. Jot down the reasons for the war, the tactics of the two sides, the successes and failures, and the outcomes.

After you've finished watching, write a paragraph for each side in the war, explaining their position. Then write a conclusion paragraph about the outcome of the war.

☺ ☺ ☺ EXPLORATION: Camp David Accords
The Camp David Accords were a peace treaty signed between Israel's Menachem Begin and Egypt's Anwar El Sadat and facilitated by U.S. President Jimmy Carter. Egypt and Israel had been in a state of war almost continuously since the formation of Israel in 1948 (Egypt immediately invaded upon hearing the news, along with Jordan and Syria).

There were two parts to the agreements made at Camp David. The first was that Israel would allow Palestinian elections to decide on the governance of the West Bank and the Gaza Strip. It was also agreed that, within five years of the elections, the Israeli military would pull out completely from these areas, leaving a Palestinian government in charge of their own autonomous land. Israel did pull out of the Gaza Strip and it is governed by Hamas today, but the West Bank is still under military governance by Israel.

The second part of the agreement was that Israel would relinquish their claims to the Sinai Peninsula and remove the Jewish settlements that had moved in since the 1967 war. Israel kept this bargain and Egypt controls the Sinai Peninsula today.

There were problems though.

1. The Golan Heights and Jerusalem were never mentioned in the Accords, leaving this land still contested today.
2. Egypt acted unilaterally, without the consent or input of any other Arab states or the Palestinians themselves, making everybody mad at Egypt and upsetting the balance of power in

Additional Layer
Israel's official stance is that they are a secular democracy, but some people say Israel is actually a theocracy.

What is a theocracy and do you think Israel is one? How can you tell? Are theocracies a bad thing or a good thing, or does it depend on the circumstances?

Famous Folks
Golda Meir was the Prime Minister of Israel during the Yom Kippur War.

She was known as "The Iron Lady." She was born in Russia and immigrated to America as a child.

Fabulous Fact

Katyusha rockets were first developed by the Soviet Union during WWII.

Photo by ChrisO at the English language Wikipedia

They are inexpensive, mobile, easy to conceal, and easy to smuggle in pieces. The rockets load onto a truck or even onto a car. They have a range of about 19 miles and can carry bombs or chemical weapons. These rockets are routinely launched at Israeli targets from Gaza, Golan Heights, Lebanon, Jordan, and the West Bank. Hezbollah fired around 4,000 of these rockets at Israel in 2006. They're not very accurate, but if your target is civilians, that's not important.

Look at a map of Israel. If you are firing from a bordering hostile area (every border, but especially Egypt right now) how far can your rockets reach? How many cities can you hit? This is why Israel is so reluctant to give up their 1967 territories. It's a matter of survival.

the Middle East as states abandoned Egypt. Iraq and Iran have since emerged as Arab/Muslim leaders in the region.

3. The Palestinians and other Arab nations are not satisfied with treaties or lands of their own to rule. They want to push Israel into the sea and kill every Jewish man, woman, and child, claiming the Holy Land for their own.

4. Some Jews still think that Israel should not have given up the entire Sinai Peninsula, which was their only source of domestic oil. Also, the Jewish settlers who were moved out of that region were angry with the plan.

5. Part of the plan also included the United States paying subsidies to both Egypt and Israel to smooth the deal. The U.S. is still paying those monies to the two nations today. Egypt receives about 1.5 billion annually. Israel receives about 3 billion annually. Both nations have used the money to build their military.

6. The UN rejected the Accords because neither they nor the Palestinians were involved. This made the part of the Accords involving the West Bank fall apart, and they were never implemented.

Color a map of Israel and surrounding nations with the borders after the Camp David Accords were signed. They are the current borders today too. You'll find a map to print at the end of this unit.

Notice on the map where the mountains are in the West Bank. To the east of the mountains lies the Jordan River in a rift valley that extends southward to the Gulf of Aqaba and beyond. If controlled by the Palestinians, the heights overlook the

crowded coastal plain of Israel and are within a few miles of striking distance of cities like Tel Aviv, even for inexpensive and readily available rockets. Also notice that the city of Jerusalem, the capital of Israel, is nearly surrounded by their enemies.

On the news today people use the term "The West Bank" to describe that region of Israel, so that's what we have used in naming the region throughout this unit. But we used the Jewish names that are still used by Israel today, Samaria & Judea, on the map. The areas of Samaria and Judea are mostly populated by Arab Palestinians, but since 1967 Jewish settlements have been established. We show a few of the Arab cities and most of the Jewish settlements.

☻ ☻ ☻ EXPLORATION: Peace in the Middle East?
David Ben-Gurion, first prime minister to Israel, said,

Why should the Arabs make peace? If I were an Arab leader I would never make terms with Israel. That is natural: we have taken their country. Sure, God promised it to us, but what does that matter to them? Our God is not theirs. We come from Israel, it's true, but two thousand years ago, and what is that to them? There has been antisemitism, the Nazis, Hitler, Auschwitz, but was that their fault? They only see one thing: we have come here and stolen their country. Why should they accept that? They may perhaps forget in one or two generations' time, but for the moment there is no chance. So, it's simple: we have to stay strong and maintain a powerful army. Our whole policy is there. Otherwise the Arabs will wipe us out.

Do you think there can be peace in the Middle East? Write a paragraph from an Israeli point of view about your terms for peace. Then write a paragraph from an Arab point of view on your terms for peace. What does each side want? How would circumstances have to change? How would attitudes have to change for there to be peace?

☻ EXPLORATION: Israel Today
Search the news for stories about Israel today. If you don't know about the places or groups the news stories talk about, look them up so you understand. Take notes on one news story and share it with your family over dinner.

☻ ☻ ☻ EXPLORATION: Israel's Prime Minister
Even though it's a small country, the prime minister of Israel is an important world leader. He or she affects the condition of the entire Middle East. Look up information together on who the prime minister of Israel is right now. Draw a portrait of him or her and then write facts about the prime minister around the portrait.

Benjamin Netanyahu

Born in Tel Aviv

Graduated from MIT in America - went to HS in America

Served as an ambassador to the U.N.

Fought in the Special Forces and was in the Yom Kippur War

Philosophies

Free-market

hard line against all terrorists

"Terrorists use the techniques of violent coercion in order to...

Has been elected Prime Minister 4 times

will not accept divided...

Additional Layer
Find out more about the PLO (Palestinian Liberation Organization). Who are they and what do they want?

Deep Thoughts
Most nations in the world say Israel is illegally occupying the West Bank which ought to belong to the PLO. But Israel says you can't occupy something that didn't belong to anybody when you took it over. The West Bank had been occupied but never given official status by the Jordanians who took it against the UN decision to make it a Palestinian State in 1948. What do you think? Is Israel in the wrong or not? Who should rule the West Bank and why?

Famous Folks
Hamas and the PLO are both considered terrorist organizations.

Can a terrorist organization legitimately rule a nation? Should they be recognized by foreign governments?

Currently Hamas is the de facto ruler of the Gaza Strip, but foreign governments regard it as belonging to a Palestinian state that doesn't actually exist right now.

GEOGRAPHY: APPALACHIAN STATES

Teaching Tip

If you are working on the Big Map project from Unit 4-1, add Tennessee, Kentucky, West Virginia, Virginia, and North Carolina to your map now.

On the Web

You can find individual maps for each of these states on Layers of Learning. http://layers-of-learning.com/geography/

Additional Layer

October Sky, a film about NASA rocket scientist Homer Hickam, is the true story of Hickam's childhood in West Virginia and a spankin' good story.

Additional Layer

West Virginia is known for its coal mines. Coal mining is still important to the state's economy in West Virginia.

Mining has been fraught with drama as well. Look up information on "West Virginia coal wars" or "Mountain Top Mining" to see some of the controversies in the past and currently.

The Appalachian states include Tennessee, Kentucky, West Virginia, Virginia, and North Carolina. Each of these states contains part of the Appalachian mountain range, which runs parallel to the Atlantic coast, north to south. The weather in these states is wet, with rain from the Atlantic Ocean and the Gulf of Mexico. They have hot summers and cool winters. The area was settled mostly by people from England, Germany, Scotland, and Switzerland.

Major industries of this region include poultry, cattle, soybeans, logging, coal mining, electrical power, textiles, banking, computer chips, horse racing, automobile manufacturing, and tourism. Jazz, bluegrass, country, Christian, and rock and roll music are all big in this region of America.

☺ ☺ ☺ **EXPLORATION: Map of the Appalachian States**
At the end of this unit you will find a map of the Appalachian region. Label and color the map with the aid of a student atlas. Older kids can handle doing more detailed maps than younger kids.

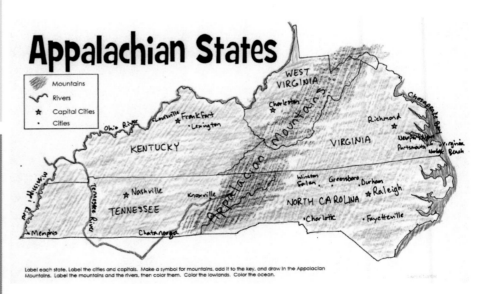

Label each state. Label the cities and capitals. Make a symbol for mountains, add it to the key, and draw in the Appalacian Mountains. Label the mountains and the rivers, then color them. Color the lowlands. Color the ocean.

☺ ☺ ☺ **EXPLORATION: Appalachian Feast**
Here are some recipes from each of the states in this unit. Choose one to make, or serve all of them together in an Appalachian feast.

<u>Kentucky Burgoo Stew</u>
This recipe reportedly was invented by a French chef just before or during the Civil War. Nowadays it's served at big horse races like the Kentucky Derby.

3-4 pounds stew meat, pork or beef
3 chicken legs, bone in
1 green pepper, chopped
1 onion, chopped
1 carrot, chopped
2 garlic cloves, diced
2 cups chicken broth
2 cups beef broth
12 oz. can diced tomatoes
1 large potato, peeled and chopped
8 oz. corn
8 oz. lima beans
4 Tbsp. Worcestershire sauce
Salt and pepper to taste

Brown the meat in hot vegetable oil until well-seared. Remove meat from pan. Add in vegetables and heat them in the oil. When vegetables are browned, add in garlic and cook for another minute. Add the liquids and remaining ingredients and return meats to the pot. Bring to a boil, then turn down the heat and simmer for two hours on low heat. Remove meat from the pot and break into smaller pieces. Remove the chicken from the bone and return to the pot in small pieces. It should be very thick when done. Serve with hot sauce.

Tennessee Spoon Bread

This recipe originated back in frontier days and is still a popular favorite in Tennessee, Kentucky, and neighboring states. And, yes, you really do eat it with a spoon.

1 cup water
1 cup yellow corn meal
2 cups milk
3 beaten eggs
1 Tbsp. sugar
1 cup creamed corn
1 Tbsp. baking powder
1 tsp. salt
2 Tbsp. melted butter
1 cup shredded sharp cheddar cheese

Bring the water to a boil, then stir in the corn meal. Stir constantly until the corn meal is cooked, about 5 minutes. Remove from heat. Add the rest of the ingredients. Stir well. Grease a 9" square baking dish and pour batter in. Bake at 375°F for 30 minutes. Eat with a spoon.

North Carolina Pork Barbecue

North Carolinians are serious about their barbecue. It's made with a tangy vinegar barbecue "mop," not the sweet tomato-based stuff you buy at the grocery store.

Pork shoulder roast
1 Tbsp. salt
¼ tsp. ground black pepper
¼ cup brown sugar
4 tsp. red pepper flakes
2 tsp. cayenne pepper
½ tsp. celery salt
½ tsp. dry mustard
½ tsp. onion powder
1 ½ cups cider vinegar

Mix the dry spices and brown sugar together and rub on the pork roast, coating it. Cover the pork roast and refrigerate overnight.

Fabulous Fact

Great Smoky Mountains National Park is located in Tennessee and North Carolina. It is the nation's most visited national park.

Additional Layer

Graceland, the home of Elvis Presley, is located in Memphis, Tennessee. For many southerners it is a must-see.

Photo by Jan Kronsell CC by SA 3.0, Wikimedia

Writer's Workshop

We include recipes from many of the states in the units of Year Four. It would be fun to create a states cookbook. You could include our recipes and others you gather.

Give it a cool cover and include notes about the recipes like where it came from.

Fabulous Fact

Tennessee is called the "Volunteer State" because during the War of 1812 thousands of Tennessee men volunteered to fight and were especially important in the Battle of New Orleans.

Additional Layer

The famous Hatfield-McCoy feud was played out in the mountains between West Virginia and Kentucky. It all started when Asa McCoy, who fought for the Union, was murdered by a Hatfield, Confederates to the core. The feud lasted a decade and involved many dramas.

Fabulous Fact

Kentucky is known as the "Bluegrass State" because of the copious amount of bluegrass that grows so well in the fertile fields.

Kentucky bluegrass has the scientific name *Poa pratensis*. It is native to Europe and parts of Asia and Africa. It's a newcomer to North America though.

Place the pork roast into a slow cooker, pour the vinegar around the pork, and cook on low for ten hours. Pull the pork apart with forks and mix the juices in. Serve on sandwich rolls with coleslaw, either on the side or on the sandwich.

Virginia Jefferson Davis Pie

Named after the Confederate president, this custard pie probably wasn't invented until the 20th century. But it's still totally Virginia.

1 cup butter, softened	2 Tbsp. flour
1 cup white sugar	1 Tbsp. vanilla extract
1 cup brown sugar	1 tsp. cinnamon
1 cup heavy cream	1 tsp. nutmeg
2 eggs	2 pie crusts, bottom crust only

Cream butter and sugars together. Add eggs and heavy cream. Blend in flour, spices, and vanilla. Stir well, until completely smooth. Pour into the two pie crusts. Bake at 350°F for 40-50 minutes until the center of the pie is set up. Let cool completely. Serve with whipped topping.

West Virginia Ramp Casserole

In West Virginia and nearby areas, they call the onions that grow wild in the hollows, ramps. So this is an onion and garlic casserole. If you don't have the wild onions, which are more pungent than the grocery store varieties, you'll just have to make do.

3 beaten eggs	½ pound sausage
5 medium potatoes, peeled and diced small	½ cup American cheese
	½ tsp. salt
6-8 ramps (or 2 grocery store onions), chopped	½ cup milk

3 cloves crushed garlic, unless you're lucky enough to have authentic ramps which don't need a garlic kicker.

Cook potatoes in a pan of water until tender. Steam ramps in a strainer over the cooking potatoes. Drain potatoes and add ramps. Fry sausage with diced garlic in a skillet, and drain off extra grease. Combine sausage with potatoes. Add eggs, diced or shredded cheese, salt, and milk. Mix and pour into a greased baking dish. Bake at 350°F for 30 minutes.

☺ ☻ EXPLORATION: Virginia Chincoteague Ponies

Off the coast of Virginia are two barrier islands: Chincoteague and Assateague. On Assateague Island there is a herd of wild ponies owned by the Chincoteague Fire Department. Every year they herd excess ponies across the water from Assateague to Chincoteague where they are auctioned off. The Chincoteague ponies are famous. Watch this video of the round-up: https://www.youtube.com/watch?v=2ulkBctY_JM

Find a "how to draw a horse" tutorial on the internet. Draw your horse on card stock and color it in. Glue blue paper waves over the horse or cut a slit in your paper so that you can pull a tab and have the water rise up the horses so they can swim like the Chincoteague ponies.

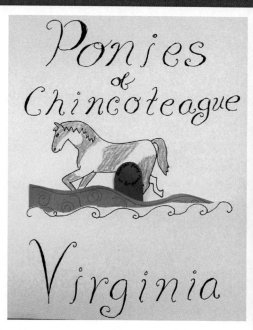

☺ ☺ ☺ EXPLORATION: Kentucky Landscape

Kentucky is a beautiful state with rolling green hills, rivers and lakes, rugged Appalachian scenery, and a lovely four season climate. Look up some images of Kentucky landscapes online then make a Kentucky landscape inspired by the images you find.

1. Observe the large blocks of color in your landscape. Dot a piece of card stock with paint in the colors of one of the blocks.
2. Scrape the paint along the card stock with the edge of an old gift card or another hard plastic piece until the whole card stock is covered with color.
3. Repeat for the remaining color blocks in your landscape.
4. Let it dry, then cut out the color blocks in the shapes of mountains, lakes, sky, fields, etc.
5. Glue the pieces together to make the whole landscape.

Famous Folks

Abraham Lincoln was born in Kentucky, a slave state, and grew to be the man who freed the slaves.

You can visit Abraham Lincoln Birthplace National Park in central Kentucky.

Additional Layer

Kentucky is mad about basketball. The Wildcats are the most successful college basketball program in history.

Make a basketball painting. Paint an orange circle on a paper and then stipple with dark orange. Let it dry, then paint on black lines for the seams in the ball. Add a University of Kentucky Logo to the painting.

On the Web

My Old Kentucky Home is an American folk song written by Stephen Foster. Listen to this version: https://youtu.be/zWI9QXBROc8

Additional Layer

Louisville slugger baseball bats are made in Kentucky.

Watch this short video about how the bats are made: https://youtu.be/uygjFpyo88U

Fabulous Fact

The Kentucky Derby is a horse race run every year in Louisville on the first Saturday in May.

On the Web

There was a song from 1941 by Harry Warren and Mack Gordon called the *Chattanooga Choo Choo*. You can watch it being performed most impressively by The Nicholas Brothers and Dorothy Dandridge to the music of the Glenn Miller Band. http://youtu.be/QzHIn5S-RbY

☺ ☺ EXPLORATION: West Virginia

West Virginia is known for its gorgeous mountain landscapes and its beautiful fall show of colors. Cut out some leaf shaped pieces of paper in red, yellow, and orange. Look up information about West Virginia and write one fact on each leaf. Glue the leaves to a piece of paper all about West Virginia.

☺ ☺ ☺ EXPLORATION: North Carolina

Read up on North Carolina and then make an advertisement poster. Choose one of these landmarks to be the feature of your poster: the Biltmore Estate, Tryon Palace, The USS North Carolina, Bellamy Mansion, Brunswick Town, or Reed Gold Mine.

☺ ☺ EXPLORATION: Chattanooga Choo Choo!

In the early 1970s, passenger train service to Chattanooga, Tennessee was stopped, and the station was almost demolished. But a group saved the property, turning it into a historical resort park with restored wood burning engines, a restored station, and a fancy hotel. The original Chattanooga Choo Choo, the nickname of the train, began service from Cincinnati in 1880.

You can read more about it here: http://choochoo.com/about/history.

You can watch this 30 minute special "Tracing the Tracks" on the Chattanooga train: https://youtu.be/fqlRqSfPU8o.

Find Chattanooga, Tennessee on a map. At the end of this unit you will find a printable Chattanooga Choo Choo. Print it onto heavy paper. Color both sides of the train, cut it out in a rough outline, and glue each side to opposite sides of a box, like a food packaging box.

☺ ☺ ☺ **EXPLORATION: State Magazine**

Pick a state from this unit and make a magazine for the state about it. Write articles about events like parades or festivals that happen in the state. Add in a recipe page. Highlight a famous person from the state in an article. Write up a destination guide for tourists with the "Top Ten" things to do in the state. Be sure to add lots of images, either drawings or photos.

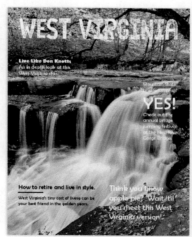

Design a magazine cover with a big attractive image and headlines for the articles inside.

This would be an excellent collaborative project for the whole family.

☺ ☺ ☺ **EXPLORATION: Penpal States**

Choose two of the states from this unit and write letters from one state to another. For example, you could have Virginia write a letter to West Virginia telling how much Virginia misses its old territory and why West Virginia should come back "home." Or you could have Kentucky write a letter telling North Carolina all about the crazy hats it saw at its last derby race.

Give the state a "voice," making it a character. Include information in your letters about the state.

Teaching Tip

If you want to do an assessment on this unit, have the kids fill out the map, states and capitals only, of the Appalachian region from memory.

Even better, have them practice drawing and labeling the map until they can do it without looking.

Additional Layer

Mammoth Cave National Park is in Kentucky. About 400 miles of the cave have been explored so far. It is believed to be the longest cave in the world.

Learn more about this cave and the Mammoth Cave National Park.

Additional Layer

If you are from the Appalachian Region, you will say "Ap-uh-latch-uh."

If you are not, you will probably say "Ap-uh-lay-shuh."

☺ ☻ ☻ EXPLORATION: Appalachian Trail

The Appalachian Trail is the longest footpath in the entire world. It's over 2,000 miles long, traversing all kinds of terrain. If you were to walk along the entire Appalachian Trail it would probably take you about seven months. You can take a tent or stay in the small shelters that are set up along the way. The trail is maintained by many volunteers who are always working to keep it free from debris and looking clean and nice. Go visit the Appalachian Trail Conservancy website to learn all about the trail. You can go visit their website and learn all about the trail, including exploring their interactive map.

On the Appalachian Trail you might just see some "trail magic." That's the name for unexpected random acts of kindness done by kind strangers, or "Appalachian Angels." These angels do things like set out chairs for tired hikers, provide a free hot dog stand along the trail, or leave little candy bars for passersby. There are even people along the trail who go out after storms to provide dry clothing.

Even if you can't go visit the trail, be an "Angel" today. Go out where you live and do some random acts of kindness for strangers to make your own "trail magic."

☺ ☻ ☻ EXPLORATION: Appalachian Stories

The people of the Appalachian region kept folk tales alive. Many of the stories had traveled from Britain and surrounding regions, but as they were told and retold many times among the mountain people of the Appalachians, they changed here and there. Still, they are often about Englishmen and stem from British and Irish history. The Jack stories, like Jack and the Beanstalk, are some of the famous ones, but there were many folktales that spread through the Appalachian region. Telling stories was their entertainment, and in the isolation of the mountains the people needed entertainment.

This particular tale, Love Like Salt, has been told countless times and many ways. Even Shakespeare told a version of it in King Lear. Read the story together, illustrate the margins, and write about what finally changed the king's mind.

Love Like Salt

An old king had three daughters. He went to town and promised to bring each what she wished. The oldest asked for a green dress, the next for a red dress, and the youngest, whom the king loved better than the others, a white dress.

When he returned he pinned a white rose on the green dress and asked the oldest how much she loved him. She said, "more than life." The second got her dress by responding, "more than words." The youngest said, "I love you like meat loves salt."

When questioned what that meant, she replied that she loved him as much as duty would allow. The king became angry and locked her in a tower on the prairie. The Duke of England rode by, saw her there, and climbed up to rescue her. The Duke took her to England as his bride.

It wasn't long before the other daughters married too. The king grew old and lonesome, and eventually he went off to live with his eldest daughter. But she scorned him and turned him away. So the old king went to his next daughter. Not wanting to be bothered, she put him in the stable to sleep.

It wasn't long before the youngest daughter and her handsome duke came. Much to their surprise, they found the king wandering around, crazy, a crown of honeysuckle vines on his head.

Then the youngest daughter brought her father home and served him a meal without salt. Her father, the king, complained. The daughter then brought out a dish of salt and stood beside her father, watching and waiting. All at once he understood her love for him. Right in his head once again, he sent his servant across the water to fetch the white dress and a whole bough of white roses, fresh as the day they were picked. At long last, the daughter had both her father's love and his reward.

On The Web

This website has English folk tales that spread to the Appalachian region as that area was settled. Over time, "royals" became "sheriffs," heroes had American values like independence and ingenuity, and the settings changed from English countrysides to mountain regions. https://perma.cc/D84Z-7AD4

Additional Layer

Here are some famous Jack tales, originating in England but spreading to the Appalachian region of the United States:

Jack and the Beanstalk

Jack Frost

Jack the Giant Killer

Little Jack Horner

This is the House that Jack Built

SCIENCE: CHEMISTRY OF FARMING

Modern farms are exponentially more productive than farms of past centuries. In fact, until the Scientific and Industrial Revolutions, farming had not changed in any significant way for thousands of years. Today many farmers have college degrees and take courses on soil structure, chemistry, plant pathology, and more.

Soil scientists examine the health of a cornfield in Missouri, USA.

Besides the massive revolution provided by mechanized equipment like tractors and harvesters, the chemical industry has changed farms more than anything else. Chemicals have increased yields by providing essential nutrients to plants. Chemicals have also reduced the destruction of crops to insects and pathogens. Farm animals are also given chemical supplements and pharmaceuticals to increase their growth and keep them healthy.

There is no doubt that these chemicals make possible much greater yields to feed the world's growing population with abundant, inexpensive food, but there are worries too. Chemicals that can kill insects can harm larger animals and people if they are ingested. Chemicals can also pollute water and kill harmless plants and animals.

☻ ☻ EXPERIMENT: Soil Chemistry
The basis for growing all crops starts in the soil. Soil that is too acidic or too basic won't grow crops well. In New England, where

leaf litter composted into the soil for thousands of years, the fields are very acidic and must be sown with lime, a base, before they are sewn with seed. In the Utah desert the soil is dry and alkaline (basic), and often farmers need to add acid supplements to the soil to balance it out before sowing crops.

1. Go outside near your house and obtain a soil sample. If you have a garden, get your sample there.
2. Place the soil in a test tube, to fill about ¼ of the test tube.
3. Fill the test tube with distilled water until it is ¾ full.
4. Now stopper the test tube and shake hard. Let it settle a bit.
5. Use a pH test strip, dipped in the water, to determine if your soil is basic or acidic or just right for plant growth.

What should you add to your soil to balance it out?

Not all plants have the same pH needs. Some actually like alkaline or acidic soil. Think about what plants you would like to put in your bit of soil and research the needs of the plants. Would your soil need to be amended before you plant?

☺ ☻ EXPLORATION: Nitrogen Fixation

Nitrogen is one of the most plentiful elements in the atmosphere of earth. It's also essential for plant and animal growth. Nitrogen is part of DNA, RNA, and proteins. But neither animals nor plants can use the nitrogen from the air directly. Plants have to get nitrogen from the soil, where it is "fixed" in ammonia (NH_3) by nitrogen fixing bacteria that live in the soil. Here is the chemical reaction that takes place:

$$N_2 + 8H^+ + 8 e^- \rightarrow 2NH_3^- + H_2$$

Nitrogen plus hydrogen (split into protons and electrons) are converted into ammonia and hydrogen gas using an enzyme called nitrogenase.

Some plants, especially legumes like peas, alfalfa, peanuts, and clover, have symbiotic bacteria that grow on their roots. These bacteria are nitrogen fixers. Often farmers will plant legumes in between other crops to replenish the nitrogen supply in their soil.

Animals have to get nitrogen by eating plants.

At the end of this unit you will find a diagram which shows the nitrogen cycle. Print it and color it.

☺ ☻ ☻ EXPERIMENT: N-P-K Nutrients for Plants

Plants need many different nutrients to grow well, just like people do, but there are three important nutrients that plants need

Fabulous Fact

In order to be an agricultural chemist you also have to understand botany, soil science, entomology, biochemistry, microbiology, genetics, and physiology.

Agricultural chemists work with the processes that determine how plants and animals grow and unitize nutrients from the environment. The goal is usually to improve or maintain crop yields and quality. Modern agricultural chemists are also concerned with sustainability. The methods they use must be healthy for the long term.

An agricultural chemist may work for an agricultural corporation, fertilizer or pesticide company, a university, or for a government.

Famous Folks

Justus von Liebig was an 19th century chemist who discovered and promoted chemical fertilizers. He used experimental methods to research farming practices.

Watch this 15 minute video about him and his work: https://youtu.be/jt3Zhd63fWY

in large amounts. These are called macronutrients. The macronutrients for plants are the elements nitrogen, phosphorus, and potassium, usually referred to by their chemical symbols, N, P, K.

Gardeners and farmers make sure their plants get the nutrients they need by fertilizing the plants. Many people use chemical fertilizers and others use manure or compost, but all do the same basic job of providing N-P-K to the plants. If you look at a bag of fertilizer from your garden store you will see three numbers separated by dashes like this: 10-10-10. The numbers represent the amount of the three major nutrients N-P-K, in that order that are in the fertilizer you see. So in a 10-10-10 fertilizer, 10% of the weight of the bag of fertilizer is Nitrogen, 10% is Phosphorus, and 10% is Potassium.

Chemical fertilizers rarely contain any nutrients other than N-P-K. They are made by taking natural ingredients, like nitrogen from the air or saltpeter from a mine, and treating them with various chemicals to get compounds rich in nitrogen, phosphorus, and potassium.

You can test how much difference chemical fertilizers make to plant growth. You'll need:

- Three identical plants
- Two different types of fertilizer, with different N-P-K ratios

1. Set all three plants in a sunny windowsill and label one "control." Label the other two with the N-P-K ratio of the fertilizer you will be adding to them.

ISRAEL - APPALACHIAN STATES - CHEM OF FARMING - MODERN MUSIC

2. Water all three plants exactly the same - at the same time and with the same amounts every day.

3. Next, add fertilizers to the plants that are labeled with their fertilizer numbers. Follow the directions on the package of fertilizer for amounts.

4. Measure the height of each plant. Measure again in a week. Measure again in two weeks. How well have your fertilized plants done in comparison to your non-fertilized plants?

What happens if you add too much fertilizer to the plants? For another experiment, compare synthetic fertilizers to compost in an experiment.

☺ ☻ ☻ EXPERIMENT: Chemistry of Compost

Compost contains the macronutrients that are also in chemical fertilizers, but not nearly as much of them. Only about 4% of the bulk of compost actually contains Nitrogen, Phosphorus and Potassium. But compost does other things that chemical fertilizers cannot. Compost provides other macro-nutrients like calcium and magnesium, and micro-nutrients like boron, iron, and copper. Compost does other things too, including amending the soil and adding bulk. It makes the structure of soil better and allows the soil to retain more moisture for plant use. In addition to this, compost encourages bacterial and fungal growth in the soil—a good thing. Bacteria and other microorganisms keep the soil healthy and produce more of the macronutrients and micro-nutrients that plants need.

When you make compost, you're not returning the spent plant materials to the soil as much as you are providing food for microorganisms. It's the microorganisms that feed your plants, not the compost directly. Microorganisms need lots of carbon to build their bodies and a little bit of nitrogen to fuel their metabolism. The ideal ratio is about 30:1. So your compost mixture should be about 30 parts carbon to every 1 part nitrogen. Plant materials that are dry and brown tend to be carbon heavy, while green and moist organic matter is nitrogen heavy.

Make your own compost in a jar. You'll need:

- A clear glass or plastic jar with a lid
- Dry leaves, paper, or old potato peels (newspaper contains lignin and takes a long time to decompose, so use it only in small amounts)
- Fresh vegetable or fruit peelings, fresh grass clippings, fresh leaves, egg shells, coffee grounds, or other parts of uncooked fruits and vegetables.

Famous Folks

Johan Gottschalk Wallerius is the father of agricultural chemistry.

He wrote the book on it in 1761 in his native Sweden.

On the Web

Cornell University has several more experiments kids can try using compost and plant growth. http://cwmi.css.cornell.edu/chapter6.pdf

Writer's Workshop

Keep a learning log during this unit to record what you are learning about farm science. As you read, experiment, discuss, and discover, keep a bulleted list of things you didn't know before that you do know now. They can even be small things, like, "I never knew that farmers went to college." You can illustrate your learning log to help you better remember what you've learned.

27

Fabulous Fact

Compost tea is water in which compost has been soaked. You place compost into an old nylon sock and let it steep in the water overnight or for several days (a warm place is best). Some people think compost tea is extra beneficial to plants. They sprinkle it over the leaves and use it to water the roots.

Can you design an experiment to show whether compost tea has benefits over traditional composting methods?

Famous Folks

Paul Hermann Mueller, a Swiss chemist, was awarded the Nobel Prize in 1948 for recognizing and applying the chemical properties of DDT to control and kill the insects that cause malaria and typhus, thereby saving the lives of millions.

- Soil from outside

1. Fill a large bowl about half full of dry, brown composting material. Now add a handful of fresh, non-dried, material.
2. Chop the brown and green materials into very small pieces. You can use a food processor if you have one.
3. Return the materials to the bowl. Add about a cup of soil from outside (or you can use purchased soil from a garden center). Add a ¼ cup of water. Mix all the materials together.
4. Fill a jar about ¾ full of your compost materials. Put several small holes in the lid of the jar and screw the lid on. Instead of the lid you can use fabric secured with a rubber band if you like.
5. Insert a thermometer into the compost jar through one of the holes.
6. Set the jar in a sunny windowsill. Once a day, turn the jar to mix up the compost and add oxygen. Once a week add a little bit more water to keep the mixture moist.

Keep an eye on your compost. How does the color and texture change over time? What happens to the temperature of the mixture? Does the temperature change when you mix up the jar or when you add water?

After your compost has completely broken down and become dark brown or black and crumbly, it's done. You can try planting a seed in the compost (or compost mixed with garden soil) and compare its growth to a seed planted only in soil.

☻ EXPLORATION: DDT

DDT stands for dichlorodiphenyltrichloroethane. This is what its chemical structure looks like:

DDT is used as a pesticide to control insects in order to save crops and to reduce the deadly pathogens that are passed on by insects, like malaria. DDT has been banned completely in the United States since 1972. It was outlawed in the rest of the world in 2001, but is still used in limited applications for control of malaria and other diseases.

When insects ingest DDT it opens up their neurons to sodium absorption, causing random firing of the synapses, giving convulsions and death. But certain individual insects are resistant to the chemical, meaning they reproduce while their unfortunate brothers die. This creates a population of mostly resistant individuals. So chemicals like DDT are only effective if they are used in a limited way.

DDT is a hydrophobic chemical, that is, it won't dissolve in or mix with water. It does like fat though, so it accumulates in the fatty tissues of animals.

DDT isn't particularly harmful to other animals or humans. If you ate a vegetable sprayed with DDT, for example, nothing would happen. In spite of textbook assertions to the contrary, no scientific link has ever been found between DDT and disease or death in either humans or animals, peregrine falcons included.

But that is an assertion on our part and you ought to do your own homework. In fact, that's your assignment. Learn more about DDT, the studies that were done about DDT, and the possible health effects it might have. Be sure you read sources who are both for and against the use of DDT. Then make up your own mind.

Fabulous Fact

Diatomaceous earth is a naturally occurring type of sedimentary rock that crumbles into a fine white powder. It is the fossilized remains of diatoms, tiny sea creatures.

When it touches the exoskeleton of an arthropod it pulls water out, killing the bug by dehydration. And so it is used as a natural insecticide.

Additional Layer

Read this article from Farm Aid on the difference between "family farms" and "factory farms." https://www.farmaid.org/issues/industrial-agriculture/what-exactly-is-a-family-farm/

Now read this short piece from Growing Georgia: http://growinggeorgia.com/news/2010/11/factory-farming-vs-family-farming/

Why do you think that farms have been tending toward large corporately controlled mega businesses? There are many reasons; see how many you can identify. What are the pros and cons of factory farms? What are the pros and cons of family farms? See what else you can find online.

Additional Layer

There are many different recipes out there for homemade "safe" weed killers.

One recipe is nothing more than boiling water poured over weeds. Salt sprinkled liberally is another. Then there's pouring vinegar over the unwanted plants.

Look up a few homemade weed killer recipes and est them scientifically to see if they perform as well as Round-up.

Teaching Tip

This unit has quite a bit of room for your student to experiment without a "recipe". Take advantage of that. If kids are always told exactly which steps to take and what the results should be they become unable to think and problem solve creatively on their own. A real scientist is very imaginative.

After they complete an experiment see if you or another student can reproduce it from their notes.

Write a persuasive essay saying why DDT should be banned or why it should not be. Cite your sources and especially the scientific studies that were done on the issue.

☻ ☻ EXPERIMENT: Glyphosate

Glyphosate is a chemical herbicide you probably know as Round-up. It works by stopping plants from producing amino acids that are necessary for plant growth. The amino acids that are interfered with are present only in plants, not in animals or humans, so the chemical cannot affect animals in the way it affects plants. Studies have found glyphosate to be non-toxic to animals and fish.

When glyphosate is sprayed on plants it is absorbed through the leaves and moves to growth points in the plant. It can take two weeks to kill the plant. The glyphosate that falls to the soil is rapidly adsorbed by (sticks to) the soil particles. It never penetrates more than 6 inches into the soil and is not washed out by water. Then it is quickly degraded by soil microbes, which metabolize it into carbon dioxide. Glyphosate completely disappears from the environment within a few weeks. However, if glyphosate ends up in surface water through erosion or because it has been sprayed on hard surfaces, like concrete or asphalt, it can be a dangerous contaminant. The bacteria that break down glyphosate are not present in sufficient quantities in aquatic environments, meaning the chemical can persist in a pond for years. Usually when surface water contamination is a problem the source of the pollution was a city environment where it was sprayed in the cracks of sidewalks or parking lots.

When people do ingest glyphosate in small amounts, such as in contaminated water, nothing happens. Your body removes the toxin in urine and expels it quickly. There are no known health risks to ingesting glyphosate, though if you purposely drink large quantities it might not be so good. The warning labels that appear on the bottle of Roundup from the store are mandated by the EPA. But glyphosate is actually a fairly safe chemical.

Do an experiment to test if glyphosate affects animals after it has been applied. Here is an experiment one kid did to compare glyphosate to "green" herbicides. http://www.virtualsciencefair. org/2012/chlysa Re-create this experiment and see if you get the same results. Or see if there are flaws in the methods and then re-do the experiment. Remember, you are trying to re-create the conditions that happen in nature, except in a controlled lab environment.

After a real scientist does an experiment he or she submits it for publication in a journal. If it is publicized, it is reviewed by peers in the scientist's field of study. Then often the experiment is done again by other scientists to see if they can re-create the results. The whole time they are looking for flaws to see if mistakes were made. This is an important part of scientific inquiry.

☺ ☺ ☺ EXPEDITION: Farm

Visit a real farm and find out what chemicals they use, if any, and what measures they take to make sure the chemical use is safe for people and the environment. Ask them if they are a family farm or a corporate farm and what the difference is. Ask them how fertilizing their farm (either with manure/compost or chemicals) increases the yields of their produce. How much of a crop would they get if they didn't fertilize at all? What else do they do to increase yields?

Find out how machines are used on the farm too. Ask how much fuels costs are and how much that affects the price of food. How and where is their food sold?

☺ ☺ ☺ EXPERIMENT: Soil Filter

Soil acts as a filter to clean contaminants out of water. This also means that contaminants can be trapped in the soil and make their way into plants, which animals and people eat. So soil filtering is a good thing, but we have to be careful about what we send into the soil in the first place.

To see how the soil filters out debris and contaminants from water, you will need:

Additional Layer

2,4-D is the short hand name of the chemical used in dozens of weed killers. It selectively kills only broad leaf plants. In other words, it kills the dandelions and clovers in your lawn, but leaves your grass alone.

It works by mimicking a growth hormone in the plant which causes out of control growth and death. That particular growth hormone is only found in certain broad leaf plants, and so it has no functional way to harm any other plant and has very low toxicity for animals and humans.

2,4-D also breaks down in the environment very quickly. Its half life is only six days in soil.

Research more about this chemical.

Additional Layer

Biochemists have developed crops that are genetically engineered to be impervious to Round-up. They call them Round-up ready crops. So a farmer could spray Round Up all over his fields without harming his crop at all.

Unfortunately, we now have glyphosate resistant plant populations in the wild too.

On the Web

At our house we have a well. We drink water straight out of the well without filters or treatment of any kind. How is it possible that water from the ground could be clean enough to drink?

Read this pdf from the Soil Science Society of America: https://www.soils.org/files/sssa/iys/april-soils-overview.pdf

Famous Folks

Sara F. Wright, a scientist for the USDA Agricultural Research Service, discovered glomalin in 1996.

Glomalin is a protein that is produced by fungi. People are still researching glomalin and how it works.

Here is an article that talks about the ongoing research: https://agresearchmag.ars.usda.gov/2002/sep/soil

Additional Layer

Some farmers now practice no-till farming. It helps prevent soil erosion, protects soil life and structure, and helps soil retain water better.

Learn how it works and if it works as well as traditional farming methods.

- A kitchen funnel
- Clear jar
- Soil
- Powdered drink mix in a dark color mixed into 2 quarts of water in a pitcher

1. Fill the funnel half full of soil.
2. Place it into the jar.
3. Pour 1/2 cup water with colored drink mix into the funnel and allow it to filter down into the jar.

Observe the color of the water in the jar. Try the experiment again and again with different types of soil (or just sand) and different thicknesses of soil. You could also filter the same water several times through the same soil and see if your water continues to get lighter in color.

☺ ☺ ☺ EXPERIMENT: Soil Glue

Soil that is undisturbed contains fungi that produce something called glomalin. Glomalin is like glue that holds the particles in the soil together. To see the effects that glomalin has on soil, you will need:

- Two clods of soil, one from an undisturbed spot and one from a spot that has been tilled or dug recently
- Two large clear jars filled with water
- Screen mesh to make a "basket" for the soil to sit in

1. Shape your mesh into a basket that dips down into the water and is secured with either a metal ring band or a rubber band.
2. Set one soil clod in each jar in the mesh basket.

Observe the results. What does glomalin do to prevent erosion? How do you think glomalin would help plant roots in soil?

If your disturbed soil sample holds together, then you either have a high clay content or you live in the Midwest United States and your soil sample is a heavy dark soil with lots of organic matter laid down centuries ago. In both cases there are physical reasons why your soil holds together apart from the presence of glomalin. Try a soil sample from another location.

☻ ☻ ☻ EXPERIMENT: Air in the Soil

Healthy soil has air in it. In fact, air is an essential ingredient in soil. Plants must have air around their roots or they suffocate. That's why if soils become waterlogged for too long, your plants will die. The bacteria, bugs, and worms that live in soil have to have air in order to live and produce the nutrients and chemicals that they produce. Not all soils have the same amounts of air.

Here is an experiment you can do to see how much air different soil samples have comparatively. You need clods of soil from several different places and some spray polyurethane.

Spray each of your soil clods with the polyurethane and give them about 5 minute to dry. Then drop each soil clod into a clear glass of water. Keep track of where each soil clod came from and whether the soil was tilled or disturbed or if it was undisturbed. You might also track whether it had been chemically treated with pesticides or fertilizers.

Air will rise from your soil clods. The longer the air bubbles are rising and the more there are, the more air was in your soil and the healthier it is.

Famous Folks

Edward H. Faulkner wrote a book in 1943 called *Plowman's Folly*. He asserted that no one had ever proposed a scientific reason for plowing. He said plowing was not only unnecessary, but harmful.

Faulkner didn't just talk about it, he produced his own test fields, using only a disk harrow to cut a furrow in which to insert his crops.

Fabulous Fact

The main soil gases are nitrogen, carbon dioxide, and oxygen. Soil organisms and plant roots must have oxygen for respiration. Plant leaves use carbon dioxide, but the roots use oxygen. CO_2 is used only for producing sugars from sunlight, but roots don't get sunlight, so they use oxygen to break down sugars, just like people do.

Other natural soil gases include radon and methane. These can leak into buildings, causing toxic environments for humans.

Also, if soil has been contaminated by industry, mining, or landfills the soil can contain gases toxic to life.

THE ARTS: MODERN MUSIC

On The Web

This short 4-minute clip, "The Differences Between The Music Genres," demonstrates a lot of the main genres of music in short musical phrases.

https://youtu.be/7ux-F9CsxW88

Fabulous Fact

This unit is about modern music, but music itself has been around since ancient times. The word "music" got its name from the Muses of Greek mythology. They were the nine daughters of Zeus who were said to inspire artists to create poems, stories, and songs. This ancient Greek pottery shows one of the Muses with a scroll.

Modern music has experienced some pretty drastic changes over the past one hundred years or so. The styles, instruments, culture, and technology associated with music have all evolved faster in this century than at any other time in the history of the world. In particular, the inventions associated with sound recordings and radio broadcasts changed the face of music by making it much more widely available. You no longer have to be wealthy enough to purchase concert or opera tickets to hear musical performances. Sound recordings are inexpensive and easy to sell and distribute. And the invention of the radio made music even more available to the masses. It wasn't long before just about everyone in developed countries was listening to songs on the radio. Now, with the internet and digital music, practically any song we want to listen to is only a few clicks away.

With this new access, the styles of music began to change. As its audience broadened, music began to be written and produced with a much bigger, more diverse audience in mind. Many popular genres and new styles emerged. Musicians became stars.

As an introduction to this unit, watch the video, "The Evolution of Popular Music by Year (1890-2009)" by MusicOutfitters to get a taste of music of the modern age and how it has evolved: https://youtu.be/GaqokusDbbs

Louis Armstrong

☺ ☺ ☺ EXPLORATION: Recording and Broadcasting

One of the main differences between modern music and the music of earlier ages is our ability to record and broadcast it. Thomas Edison made the very first sound recording in 1877 with his invention of the phonograph. It wasn't long before Heinrich Hertz and Guglielmo Marconi were sending out radio waves. By the 1920s, listening to the radio was a form of entertainment. In the past century we've improved on sound quality, broadcasting, and storage. Imagine how many records, 8 tracks, or cassettes it would take to hold all the songs you can store on your phone or i-Pod.

Choose four of these musical inventions to create a quadrama about (instructions at http://layers-of-learning.com/quadrama/). Put one invention on each of the four sections of the quadrama. Include a picture of the invention along with some caption boxes about the inventor, how the invention works, and how it has changed the music industry.

- phonograph
- microphone
- headphones
- cassette tapes
- 8 track tapes
- Vocoder
- transistor radio
- Sony's Walkman
- compact disc
- auto-tuners
- MP3 players
- iPods

☺ ☺ EXPLORATION: Tin Pan Alley

Nowadays most musicians and their songs are discovered by the recordings they make. Their recorded music is heard by producers, and then the lucky ones get a chance to sign on with a label. New songs are heard far and wide on the radio, and pretty soon we're all singing and playing along. But before sound recordings were so easy to make, American musicians went to Tin Pan Alley. It was a stretch of road in New York City where quite a few song publishers had set up shop. Musicians were hired as "pluggers" to play the new songs for the publishers and the crowds on the street, to see what was popular and what was worth publishing. They were called "pluggers" because they were trying to plug, or promote, the new songs. The best songs would be turned into sheet music and sold. Tin Pan Alley got its name because there were so many pianos playing all at the same time that it sound-

On The Web

Watch the "Top 10 Unbelievable Facts in Music History" by WatchMojo. com:

https://youtu.be/aZj-od5zdYWk

Additional Layer

Along with the Industrial Revolution came the piano. Piano sales were on the rise the 19th and 20th centuries in America and Europe. People were enrolling in piano lessons and there were pianos in many homes. It was this trend that created the need for Tin Pan Alleys, which primarily produced sheet music that was for sale. This painting, *Girls at the Piano*, was made by Renoir.

On The Web

Did you know there's another "Tin Pan Alley" in London? Watch "Tin Pan Alley (1951)" by British Pathe to learn more.

https://youtu.be/xQkIB-MIt-Pg

Additional Layer

West Side Story used a unique concept. It took Shakespeare's famous play, *Romeo and Juliet*, and turned it into a modern, updated story set in New York City. Rather than Elizabethan families, the Montagues and Capulets were rival gangs called the Jets and the Sharks. The live stage show ended up being turned into a movie that won two Academy Awards.

Famous Folks

Here are some jazz musicians you should know:

Louis Armstrong

Duke Ellington

Bessie Smith

Billie Holiday

Benny Goodman

Glenn Miller

Charlie Parker

Miles Davis

ed like tin pans clashing and banging together in a cacophony of sound.

Make your own tin pan alley by gathering some people and creating your own sounds. You can use real or homemade instruments. Craft a sign that says "Tin Pan Alley" to hang up at your entrance. Have everyone come inside the alley and find either instruments or some materials to make instruments. Use pie plates, shakers, coffee can drums, water glasses, or any other instruments or sound makers you have. Everyone can play their own song all at the same time. That's what it was like at Tin Pan Alley, with everyone playing and vying for attention.

Watch this little video, "Tin Pan Alley Times" by Michael J. Miles, to hear some of the songs and history of Tin Pan Alley: https://youtu.be/udd4-9oQChc.

☺ ☺ ☺ EXPLORATION: Jazz

Jazz music has an interesting heritage. In parts of Louisiana the black slaves of the day were allowed to take Sundays off from their work. They gathered together in public squares or other meeting places to socialize. It wasn't long before the city restricted their gatherings though, and allowed them only to meet in one clearing, which came to be known as Congo Square. They began meeting there to talk, sing, play music, and

Famous Jazz singer, Billie Holiday

dance. Many Africans immigrated to the area and the culture there took on a uniquely African feel. These gatherings became the birthplace of jazz music.

The new music style was a combination of the rhythms of African music with the instruments of the Western world. The musicians often just felt the music and words, making it up spur of the moment as they played in the streets of New Orleans. For a long time people tried to put a stop to the gatherings at Congo Square. They even renamed it so it would lose some of its notoriety.

Today people are trying to preserve its history, and if you go there on a Sunday, you can still watch the dancing and hear the music of Congo Square. Jazz musicians gather on street corners, singing

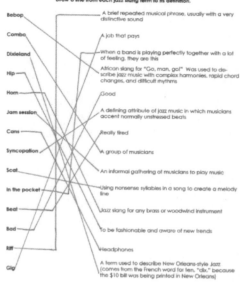

Do You Speak Jazz?
Draw a line from each jazz slang term to its definition.

Bebop
Combo
Dixieland
Hip
Horn
Jam session
Cans
Syncopation
Scat
In the pocket
Beat
Bad
Riff
Gig

A brief repeated musical phrase, usually with a very distinctive sound

A job that pays

When a band is playing perfectly together with a lot of feeling, they are this

African slang for "Go, man, go!" Was used to describe jazz music with complex harmonies, rapid chord changes, and difficult rhythms

Good

A defining attribute of jazz music in which musicians accent normally unstressed beats

Really tired

A group of musicians

An informal gathering of musicians to play music

Using nonsense syllables in a song to create a melody line

Jazz slang for any brass or woodwind instrument

To be fashionable and aware of new trends

Headphones

A term used to describe New Orleans-style Jazz (comes from the French word for ten, "dix," because the $10 bill was being printed in New Orleans)

play the matching game. http://bit.ly/2s4e7Lw

😊 😊 😊 **EXPLORATION: Musicals**
Musicals emerged in the 1920s, but they became a really popular form of entertainment beginning in 1943 when *Oklahoma* came out. Song and dance numbers were incorporated into live shows and movies that helped drive the storyline along. Many people still flock to theaters to see live Broadway shows.

Musicals have two basic elements:

1. Libretto - This means "the book" and refers to the narrative structure that keeps the story going in between the songs. People connect with the characters through the story.
2. The Score - This is the song part of the musical. At least half is dedicated to the song-and-dance portion. This is where character development occurs and we hear the thoughts, struggles, and plans of the characters through their songs. Songs happen at exciting or emotional moments within the story.

Watch one of these famous musicals to experience it firsthand:
- *Show Boat*
- *Oklahoma!*
- *Singin' in the Rain*
- *White Christmas*
- *My Fair Lady*
- *West Side Story*
- *Fiddler On The Roof*
- *Cats*

and playing for passersby.

Jazz music developed its own slang. While you listen to some jazz music, use the "Do You Speak Jazz?" printable from the end of the unit to play a matching game of jazz slang. There are hundreds of jazz slang terms, many of which we still use today, so if you're interested you can find lots more online.

Listen to the "Top 100 Jazz Classics Playlist" by Electronics USA on YouTube. You can listen while you

Famous Folks

Richard Rodgers and Oscar Hammerstein were the team that created *Oklahoma!* They made many popular musicals. *The Sound of Music* was the last one they made together. It was made into a film and has more hit songs than any of their other productions.

Additional Layer

Types of songs you can watch for in musicals include:

ballads

comedies

musical scenes (a combination of singing and dialogue)

finale (often many characters join together for this final number)

Writer's Workshop

Choose a favorite song that you love and think of it like the writer of a musical production would if it were in your musical. Who is singing and what is his or her story? Where is the story taking place? What is the main problem to overcome?

Write the story of the song.

Famous Folks

Michael Jackson was a famous singer, called the King of Pop. He had a controversial life, but produced some iconic songs like *Beat It, Thriller, Billie Jean, and Bad.* He was known not only as a great singer and songwriter, but also revolutionized music videos and introduced dancing as an important part of a singer's act. He will always be remembered for his famous moon walk.

- *Les Miserables*
- *Phantom of the Opera*
- *Hamilton*

As you watch, notice the basic elements of a musical.

☺ ☺ ☺ EXPLORATION: The Blues

Blues singers are known for singing sad songs. They sing about hard times, troubles, and broken hearts. It all started with the enslaved Africans of the Deep South who were singing about their misery and hard times. They often included a good mix of hope, strength, and humor too. And they had a very distinct rhythm.

Listen to the great B.B. King singing "Got The Blues."

https://youtu.be/WFr_q5odUfQ

Most blues tunes are built on just three chords and 48 beats, or 12 bars that each have four beats in them. A bar is just a measure of time. Clap evenly four times in a row. You've just clapped a bar. For the blues, you need 12 bars, so you'll clap 12 sets of 4 claps. To help you keep track of the sets you can alternate between bars of clapping your hands, snapping your fingers, patting your knees, and stomping your feet. If you do three rotations of those bars, you will have kept a beat for all 12 bars. Give it a try.

Often blues songs were improvised, or created right on the spot. Improvise your own Blues song. Keep your 12 bar rhythm going while you sing your own sad song to it. Here are some sad topics to inspire you:

Doing the Dishes Blues

Early Bedtime Blues

Grounded from TV Blues

Bike Has A Flat Tire Blues

Been Rainin' For 3 Days Blues

My Dog Died Blues

Too Many Chores Blues

☺ ☺ ☺ EXPLORATION: Rock and Roll Rhythms

When rock and roll was new it took the world by storm. It was a combination of a lot of styles all fused into one new sound; gospel, blues, jazz, boogie woogie, and country music all joined up to make the new style. The guitar began to emerge as the lead instrument in bands and an upbeat, happy rhythm had everyone clapping along to it.

Get a drum (or a pot with some spoons) and try out this rock and roll rhythm. We'll start with a basic beat and then turn it into a rock and roll beat. Use your drum to keep this time, playing on every number and on the "ands."

1 and 2 and 3 and 4 and 1 and 2 and 3 and 4 and . . .

Now we'll add some rock and roll by playing the stressed beats extra loud. The stressed beats are bold. If you practice you might be able to play the stressed beats loudly with both drumsticks at once, while playing with only one drumstick at a time on the un-stressed beats.

1 and **2** and 3 and **4** and 1 and **2** and 3 and **4** and . . .

☺ ☻ EXPLORATION: Elvis Presley

Elvis Presley may just have made the biggest international impact of any musician. He introduced the world to Rock and Roll and popularized the style that led to so many new genres of music. He legendary hip swivel and exciting performances had crowds following him, and he is still popular and recognizable long after his death.

Go explore www.elvis.com. Explore the "About" and "Music" tabs. You can read his bio, peruse an Elvis time line, and listen to samples of his music. Use the Elvis Presley Fact Sheet Printable to write down lots of facts you found out as you read about the King of Rock and Roll.

☺ ☺ ☻ EXPLORATION: Beatlemania

The songs of John Lennon, Paul McCartney, George Harrison, and Ringo Starr were so full of life that their band, The Beatles, revolutionized music throughout much of the world. The music of the 1960s was making headlines. Reporters followed the four teenagers. Fans followed them everywhere, and people mimicked their music, clothing, style, and even their hair. They were nick-

Writer's Workshop

Write a journal entry in your writer's notebook. If you could play any musical instrument in the world really well, which one would it be?

Tell about why you chose that instrument and what you would do with that talent if you had it.

Fabulous Fact

Elvis is known for his many famous songs, but he didn't actually write any of them. He was a singer, but not a song-writer.

Additional Layer

We tend to know famous singers, but there are a lot of people behind the scenes too. Composers, musicians, producers, sound technicians, and many others all play a role in a song becoming successful.

Philip Glass is a modern composer who has written everything from operas to film scores. He's won Golden Globes, Academy Awards, and other honors, but chances are, you've never heard of him because his name isn't in lights.

Additional Layer

Certain songs can be merged together because they share the same counterpoint.

Gather a few friends and have each one sing a different song at the same time to the same beat. If they have the same counterpoint, it will sound like the melodies go perfectly together. Get together with a few friends and try singing two of these songs that share the same counterpoint at the same time. You have to keep the same beat.

Row, Row, Row Your Boat

Three Blind Mice

Are You Sleeping?

Down By The Station

Use "la-las" instead of the words so your words don't muddy together.

Fabulous Fact

In 1964 the Beatles had songs in each of the top 5 spots on the charts. No one else has ever accomplished that.

Fabulous Fact

None of the Beatles could read music. They just played by ear.

named "the Moptops" because of their long hair. Others called them the "Fab Four."

Their concerts were unlike anything before. Policemen and ambulances always had to be ready at their concerts in case the screaming, adoring fans got out of hand. Still today, they are the most celebrated band in history.

Part of their success stems from the hope their music brought to a devastated post-World Wars world. In 1964, when the Beatles blasted their way on to the music scene, times felt uncertain. The aftermath of the wars still had people reeling from the losses and turmoil. Vicious dictators had risen to power. The atomic bombs had been dropped. So many had died. After the wars, the social, political, and cultural tides were turning and women and minorities were demanding more rights and equal pay. The Beatles brought positivity and hope to a world that badly needed it. Their joyful, upbeat songs were a welcome respite from the harshness of the world. And their irreverence, long hair, and attitudes gave youth courage to stand up and be whoever they wanted to be. Perhaps without meaning to, they introduced teen rebellion in a new and widespread way.

Watch this short clip called "1964: America Experience":

https://youtu.be/JpGaLtC9lFI

Listen to some Beatles songs while you make the Beatles finger puppets using the printable from the end of this unit.

Writer's Workshop

The Beatles empowered young people to stand up to their elders. A lot of the older generation didn't approve of their music, their long hair, or their message.

Write about why celebrities have such a strong influence on young people. Do you think its a positive or a negative thing? Can it be both? Who influences you?

☺ ☺ ☺ EXPEDITION: Electrifying Music

As soon as electricity got involved, music seemed to become louder. Microphones pick up the sound waves and convert them into electrical signals. An amplifier strengthens the sound. Then finally, speakers change the signals back into sound waves which are broadcast out for all to hear. Now instead of holding a concert for a few people on a small stage, we can blast concerts to thousands of people in huge concert halls or even outdoors.

Instruments can also be plugged right into amplifiers to make their sound louder. An electric guitar really gave rock and roll music its signature sound. Most rock bands have several electric guitar players.

Additional Layer

Faster modes of transportation like airplanes and cars has also made it possible for musicians to travel around, putting on concerts and seeing their fans.

Make arrangements with a music store to take a tour. Often you'll be able to try out many of the instruments, including some like electric guitars and keyboards that can be amplified. Most music store owners are musicians themselves, so you may even get to hear them play for you a little. Come prepared with some questions to ask about instruments, musical styles, or modern music.

Fabulous Fact

A Canadian astronaut and singer who was living on the International Space Station released an album that he recorded entirely in space in 2015. His name was Chris Hadfield and his album was called *Space Sessions: Songs From A Tin Can*.

Famous Folks

Johnny Cash was a country music star known for his deep voice. Country music is centered in Nashville, Tennessee, and that's where Johnny lived and worked. He, like many celebrities, tried to use his fame and fortune to influence the world. Here he is meeting with U.S. President Nixon about prison reform.

On The Web

Do you want to make your own little music video, but you don't have the extra people or costumes? You can pop your face into a JibJab clip and watch your silly self dance and sing. You have to pay for an account to save the video, but anyone can watch on their site for free. Most of the clips are appropriate, but a few are questionable, so parents should preview. The site has instructions for inserting your photos. Be prepared to laugh.
www.jibjab.com/

☻ ☻ ☻ EXPLORATION: Explosion of Genres

With the coming of modern music came a lot of new styles and genres. Here are just a few of the styles that emerged.

- Jazz
- Rock and Roll
- Disco
- Country
- Bluegrass
- Folk
- Gospel
- Rap
- Rhythm and Blues
- Punk
- Opera
- Musical

Write down each of these modern musical genres on slips of paper and put them into a bowl or a hat. Play a game with them by taking turns drawing them out of the hat, one at a time. Choose a simple song you know, like *Row, Row, Row Your Boat* or *Twinkle, Twinkle Little Star*. Try to sing the song in the style of the genre you drew out. Take turns transforming the song into each genre until you've tried them all. You might need to get online and listen to some of the styles that are less familiar to you first.

☻ ☻ ☻ EXPLORATION: Music Videos

Music videos are often made to go with new popular songs. As the song plays, you watch the singer dance and act out scenes that explain more about what the song means and what its back story is. Go online and watch some music videos. **(Parents, please preview and make sure the videos you choose are appropriate for your kids.)** Just go to YouTube and search for a popular modern song you really like, and see if there was a video made for it.

Notice how the videos are often made collage-style. The scenes change frequently. There are often many costume changes too. You'll likely see lots of backup dancers and singers too. Did the music video change your perception of what the song was about at all?

You can just watch several music videos, or you can try to make your own. Get a group of kids together and choose a song everyone is familiar with. Just play the song loudly while lip syncing, dancing, and acting out parts of the song. It's a lot more fun if you have some silly costumes and pretend microphones or other instruments.

☻ ☻ ☻ EXPLORATION: Making Music With Machines

Most of the songs you hear on the radio today weren't just simply recorded once. They were produced in a music recording studio over many takes. That's called multi-track recording. Record producers record many parts of a song separately and then overdub lots of vocal and instrumental tracks all together into one song. One singer can even sing several parts, like a melody line and a harmony line, and those can be put together into one track.

Along with multi-track recording, sound mixing, and auto-tuning, other editing techniques have also given music a lot of new sounds. Go visit https://you.dj/ and do a little sound mixing of your own. You can begin by selecting a genre and then songs. Start playing with all of the options, adding a drumbeat, looping, or creating an echo. You can even combine the sounds of two songs into one. The website has a help section if you decide you want to do more than just experiment and play with the sounds.

Fabulous Fact

Have you ever had a song that got stuck in your head? The actual term for that is an earworm.

Additional Layer

Soundtracks have become big business in the modern music realm. A soundtrack is the music that runs during a movie. Because of the prevalence of the film industry, many songs have gained massive popularity by their inclusion in a movie. Many instrumental soundtracks make great study music, so if your kids like tunes while they study, visit youTube and search for movie soundtracks playlists. *Wonderful Movie Soundtracks* by AtomE+ is a great one.

Coming up next . . .

Unit 4-15

Cold War
U.S. Territories
Chemistry of Medicine
Free Verse

My ideas for this unit:

Title: _____ **Topic:** _____

_____

_____

_____

_____

_____

_____

_____

_____

_____

_____

Title: _____ **Topic:** _____

_____

_____

_____

_____

_____

_____

_____

_____

_____

_____

Title: _____ **Topic:** _____

_____

_____

_____

_____

_____

_____

_____

_____

_____

_____

Title: _____ **Topic:** _____

_____
_____
_____
_____
_____
_____
_____
_____
_____
_____
_____

Title: _____ **Topic:** _____

_____
_____
_____
_____
_____
_____
_____
_____
_____
_____
_____
_____

Title: _____ **Topic:** _____

_____
_____
_____
_____
_____
_____
_____
_____
_____
_____
_____

Israel in the Middle East

This is a soldier of the Israeli armed forces. He is wearing a phylactery on his head and reading from his holy book. Not all Israelis are religious, but they all have to defend their way of life every day.

Modern Israel Timeline

1900s
Persecuted Jews purchase land and begin moving to the Ottoman-controlled Holy Land

1909
Tel Aviv is founded as a Jewish city

1917
Balfour declaration creates a Jewish homeland; Arabs launch terrorist attacks and side with Hitler

1945-1948
Illegal Israel immigrants, mostly Holocaust survivors, are held in British internment camps

1947
Partition of Israel by the UN

1948
David Ben-Gurion is elected first Prime Minister of Israel

1948-1951
700,000 Jews immigrate to Israel

1950
Law of Return; all Jews throughout the world can claim Israeli citizenship if they wish

1958
Israel's population reaches 2 million, almost all newcomers were destitute, straining the resources

1960
By this time nearly all Jews from Arab states had fled to Israel or America, more than 850,000

1966
America begins to supply weapons to Israel and becomes Israel's strongest supporter

June 1967
Six-Day War; Israel dominates

David Ben-Gurion

He first immigrated to the Holy Land in _____ when it was still owned by the Ottoman Turks.

When he was a young man he went to school at _____.

During the second World War Ben-Gurion supported the _____.

He was head of the _____ political party, which was left leaning socialist.

He set up Israel as a secular democratic state with free elections and freedom of speech and religion.

David Ben-Gurion was born in the country of _____ in the year _____.

During World War I he fought on the side of the _____.

He led Israel in the 1948 _____ war.

He became head of the _____ which was the agency responsible for the immigration and gathering of the Jews to the Holy Land.

Record of Jewish Expulsion and Persecution

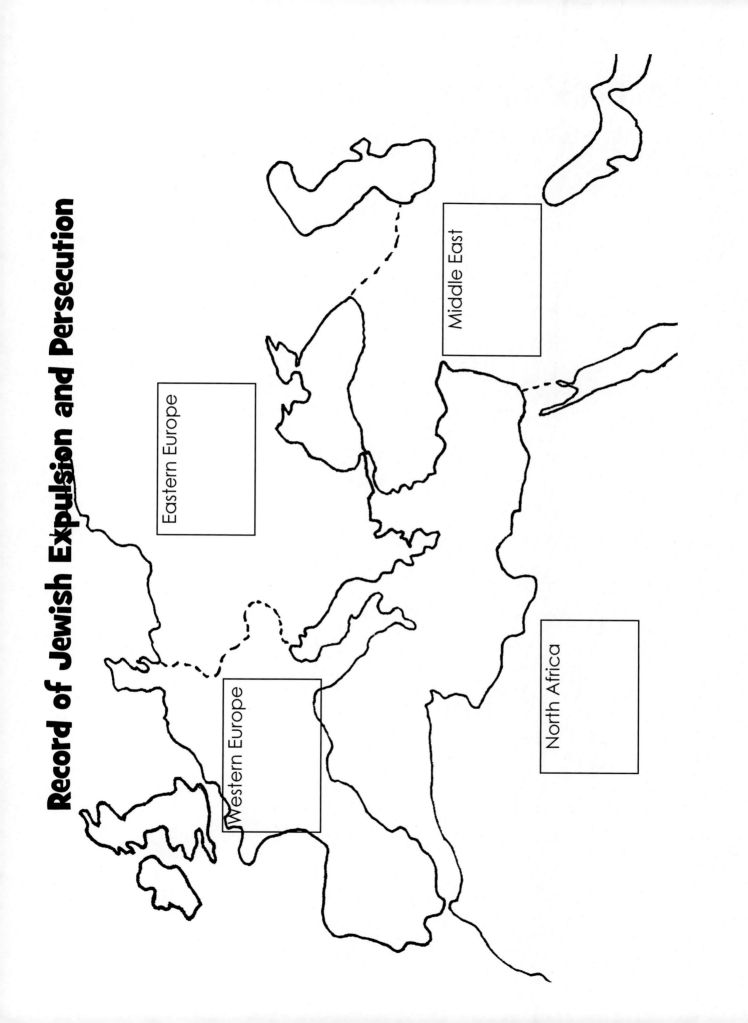

Eastern Europe

Middle East

Western Europe

North Africa

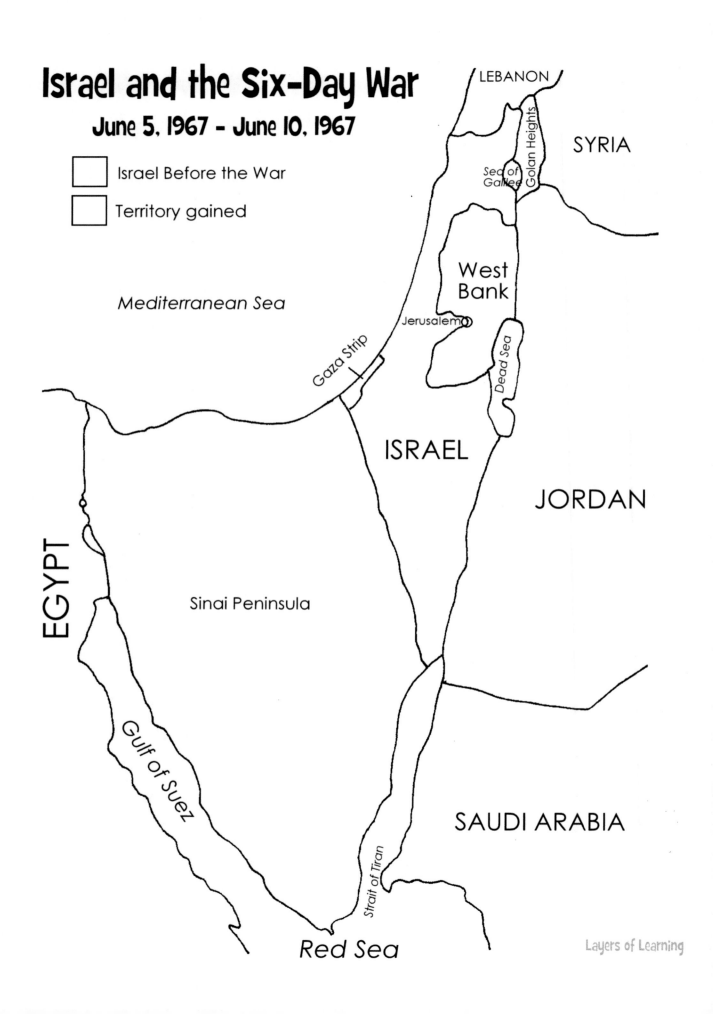

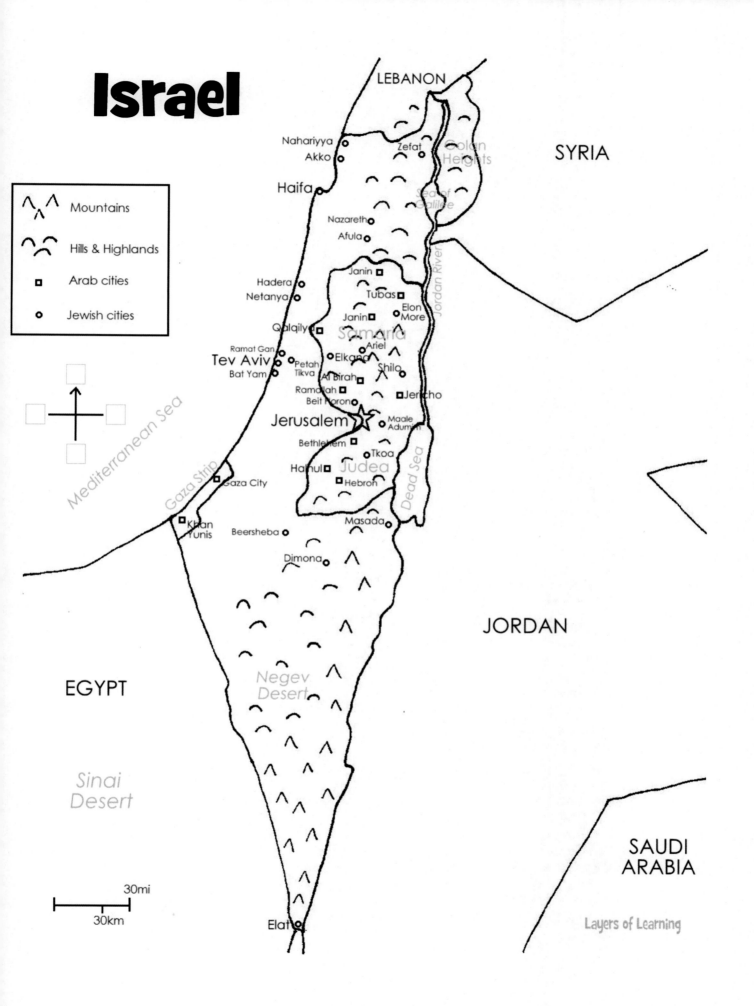

Israel

Mountains

Hills & Highlands

☐ Arab cities

○ Jewish cities

LEBANON

SYRIA

Nahariyya
Akko
Zefat
Golan Heights

Haifa

Sea of Galilee

Nazareth
Afula

Janin
Tubas
Elon More
Janin
Qalqilya
Samaria
Ariel
Ramat Gan
Elkana
Tev Aviv
Petah Tikva
Shilo
Bat Yam
Al Birah
Ramallah
Beit Horon
Jericho
Jerusalem
Maale Adumin
Bethlehem
Tkoa
Halhul
Judea
Gaza Strip
Gaza City
Hebron
Khan Yunis
Beersheba
Masada

Jordan River

Dead Sea

Mediterranean Sea

Dimona

JORDAN

EGYPT

Negev Desert

Sinai Desert

SAUDI ARABIA

30mi

30km

Elat

Layers of Learning

Appalachian States

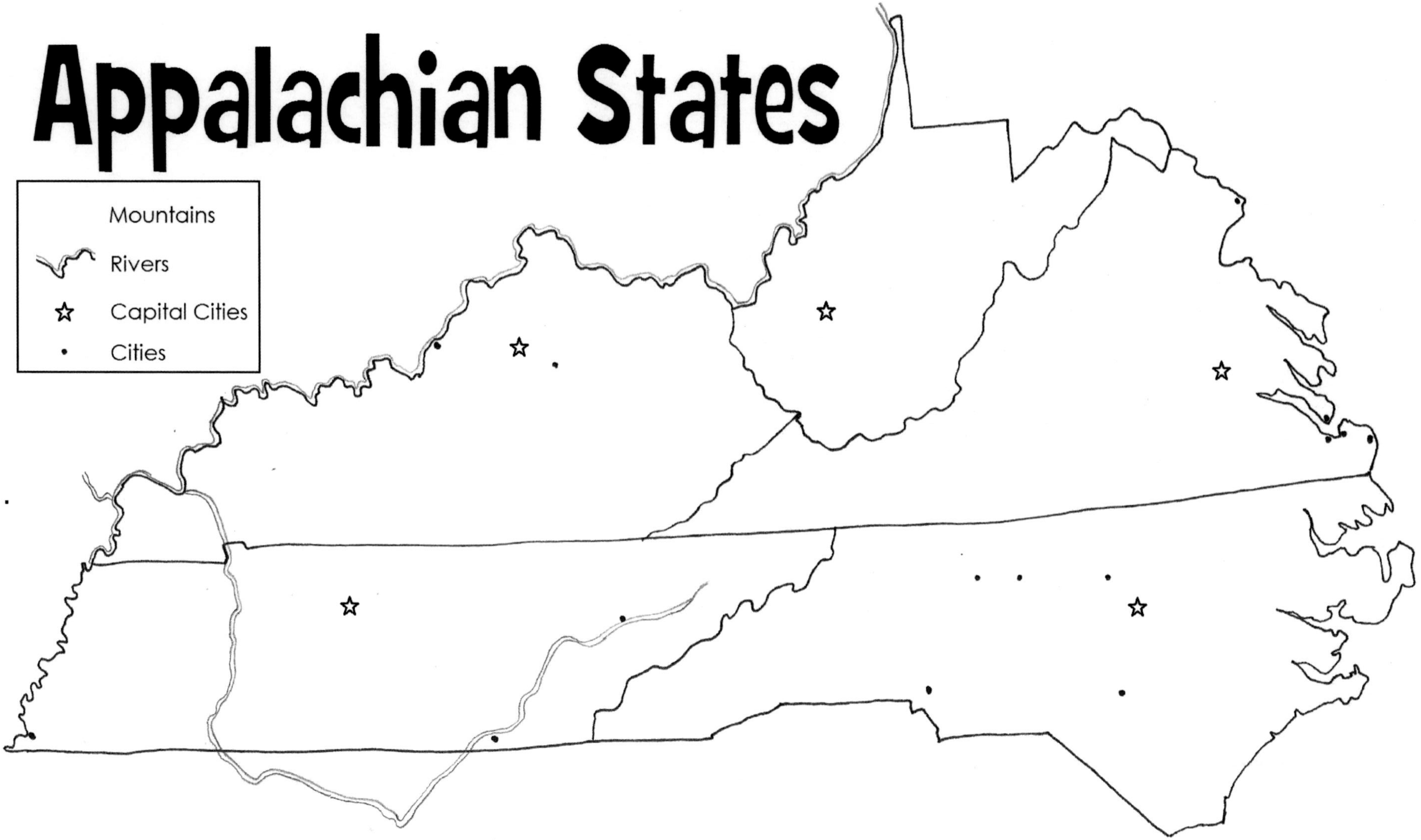

Key:

~ Mountains

∿ Rivers

☆ Capital Cities

• Cities

Label each state. Label the cities and capitals. Make a symbol for mountains, add it to the key, and draw in the Appalacian Mountains. Label the mountains and the rivers, then color them. Color the lowlands. Color the ocean.

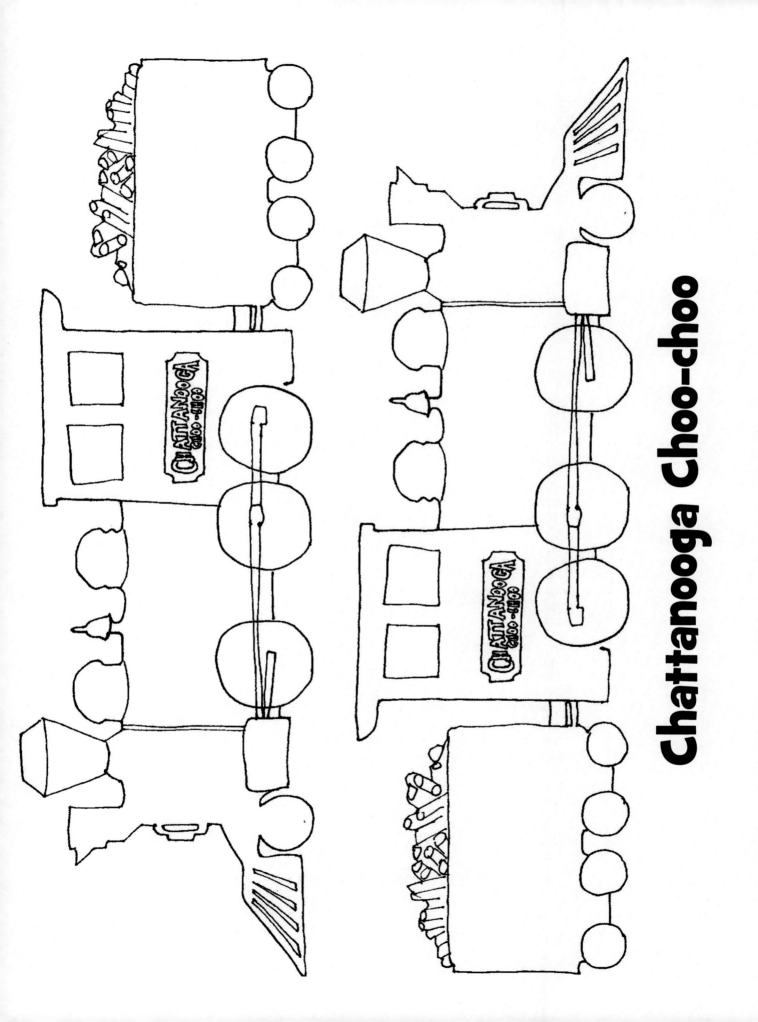

Chattanooga Choo-choo

Love Like Salt

An old king had three daughters. He went to town and promised to bring each what she wished. The oldest asked for a green dress, the next for a red dress, and the youngest, whom the king loved better than the others, a white dress.

When he returned he pinned a white rose on the green dress and asked the oldest how much she loved him. She said, "more than life." The second got her dress by responding, "more than words." The youngest said, "I love you like meat loves salt."

When questioned what that meant, she replied that she loved him as much as duty would allow. The king became angry and locked her in a tower on the prairie. The Duke of England rode by, saw her there, and climbed up to rescue her. The Duke took her to England as his bride.

It wasn't long before the other daughters married too. The king grew old and lonesome, and eventually he went off to live with his eldest daughter. But she scorned him and turned him away. So the old king went to his next daughter. Not wanting to be bothered, she put him in the stable to sleep.

It wasn't long before the youngest daughter and her handsome duke came. Much to their surprise, they found the king wandering around, crazy, a crown of honeysuckle vines on his head.

Then the youngest daughter brought her father home and served him a meal without salt. Her father, the king, complained. The daughter then brought out a dish of salt and stood beside her father, watching and waiting. All at once he understood her love for him. Right in his head once again, he sent his servant across the water to fetch the white dress and a whole bough of white roses, fresh as the day they were picked. At long last, the daughter had both her father's love and his reward.

What finally changed the king's mind?

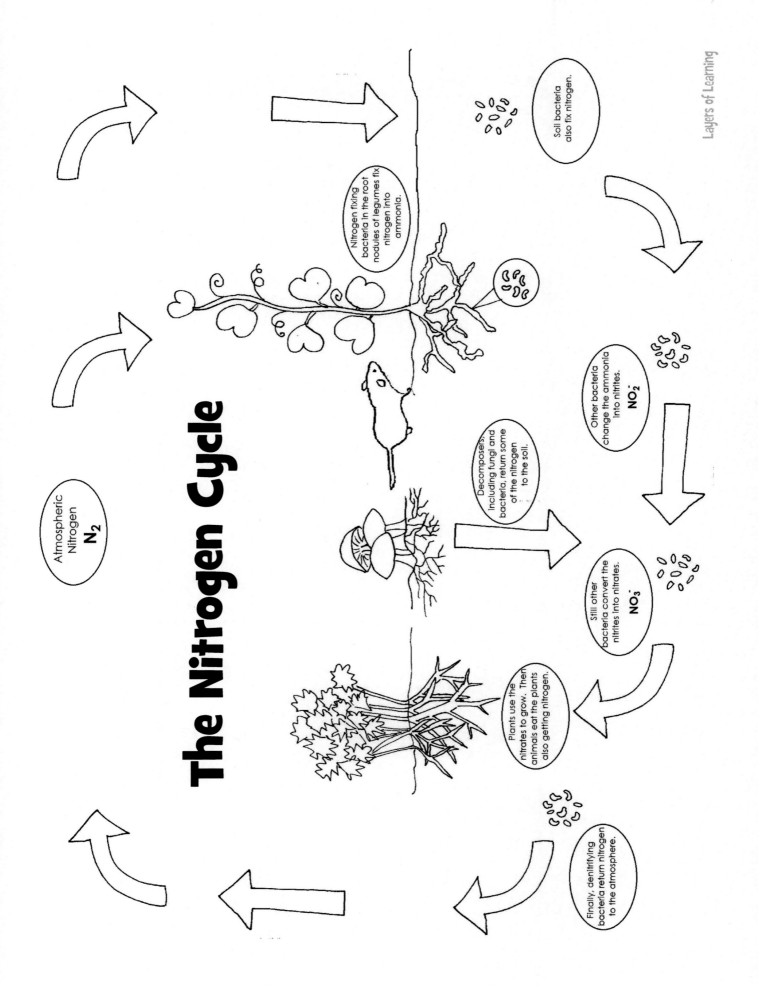

The Nitrogen Cycle

Atmospheric Nitrogen
N_2

Nitrogen fixing bacteria in the root nodules of legumes fix nitrogen into ammonia.

Soil bacteria also fix nitrogen.

Other bacteria change the ammonia into nitrites.
NO_2^-

Still other bacteria convert the nitrites into nitrates.
NO_3^-

Decomposers, including fungi and bacteria, return some of the nitrogen to the soil.

Plants use the nitrates to grow. Then animals eat the plants also getting nitrogen.

Finally, denitrifying bacteria return nitrogen to the atmosphere.

Do You Speak Jazz?

Draw a line from each Jazz slang term to its definition.

Bebop   A brief repeated musical phrase, usually with a very distinctive sound

Combo   A job that pays

Dixieland   When a band is playing perfectly together with a lot of feeling

Hip   African slang for "Go, man, go!" Was used to describe jazz music with complex harmonies, rapid chord changes, and difficult rhythms

Horn   Good

Jam Session   A defining attribute of Jazz music in which musicians accent normally unstressed beats

Cans   Really tired

Syncopation   A group of musicians

Scat   An informal gathering of musicians to play music

In the Pocket   Using nonsense syllables in a song to create a melody line

Beat   Jazz slang for any brass or woodwind instrument

Bad   To be fashionable and aware of new trends

Riff   Headphones

Gig   A term used to describe New-Orleans-style Jazz (comes from the French word for ten ("dix") because the $10 bill was being printed in New Orleans

Elvis Presley Fact Sheet

The Beatles Finger Puppets

JOHN

PAUL

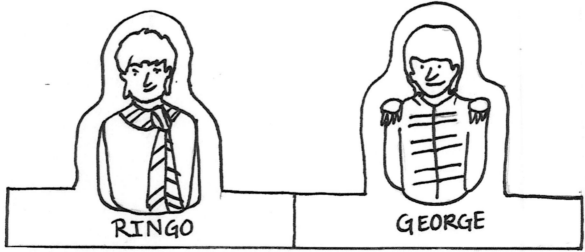

RINGO

GEORGE

About the Authors

Karen & Michelle . . .
Mothers, sisters, teachers, women who are passionate
about educating kids.
We are dedicated to lifelong learning.

Karen, a mother of four, who has homeschooled her kids for more than eight years with her husband, Bob, has a bachelor's degree in child development with an emphasis in education. She lives in Idaho, gardens, teaches piano, and plays an excruciating number of board games with her kids. Karen is our resident arts expert and English guru {most necessary as Michelle regularly and carelessly mangles the English language and occasionally steps over the bounds of polite society}.

Michelle and her husband, Cameron, have homeschooled their six boys for more than a decade. Michelle earned a bachelors in biology, making her the resident science expert, though she is mocked by her friends for being the Botanist with the Black Thumb of Death. She also is the go-to for history and government. She believes in staying up late, hot chocolate, and a no whining policy. We both pitch in on geography, in case you were wondering.

Visit our constantly updated blog for tons of free ideas,
free printables, and more cool stuff for sale:
www.Layers-of-Learning.com

Made in the USA
Middletown, DE
04 April 2025

73769542R00035